THE GOSPEL OF MARK

THE GOSPEL OF MARK

A Study Manual

by
HERSCHEL H. HOBBS

BAKER BOOK HOUSE
Grand Rapids, Michigan

Library of Congress Catalog Card
Number: 75-156743
ISBN: 0-8010-4017-5

Second printing, July 1978

PHOTOLITHOPRINTED BY CUSHING - MALLOY, INC.
ANN ARBOR, MICHIGAN, UNITED STATES OF AMERICA
1978

DEDICATION

to

W. A. CRISWELL

my friend through the years and a mighty preacher of the Gospel of Jesus Christ

INTRODUCTION

It is generally agreed that this Gospel was written by John Mark, whose mother was a woman of distinction among the early Christians (cf. Acts 12:12). Her home seems to have been the gathering place for the early Christians in Jerusalem, and may have been the place where Jesus ate the last passover meal with His disciples. Such would bring Mark into connection with many of the events recorded in this Gospel.

Through his mother he was related to Barnabas (Col. 4:10; cf. Acts 12:25; 15:39). Since Peter calls him "Marcus my son" (I Peter 5:13) it is possible that Peter had won him to Christ. Certainly he was a co-laborer with Peter, as well as Barnabas and Paul (cf. Acts 12:25—13:13; 15:39; Philem. 24; II Tim. 4:11).

"Mark" (Marcus) was a Roman name; "John" was a Hebrew name. Whether this Roman name has any relation to the writing of this Gospel is open to question. But it is generally agreed that he wrote it with Roman readers in mind. It is possible that he wrote it in Rome, though this is not certain. But the contents and style reflect readers who were not familiar with Aramaic, the language of the Jews in the first century. The emphasis upon Jesus' actions, as over against His teachings, suggests readers such as the Romans whose primary interests were with deeds not words. Mark uses colloquial Greek (Moule, *The Gospel According to Mark,* "Cambridge Bible Commentary," University Press, 1965, p. 3), but his account is moving and vivid. He made great use of the historical present tense and the imperfect tense which reflect action. His plentiful use of *euthus* (immediately or straightway) shows Jesus moving quickly from one action to another.

This Gospel reflects an eye-witness source. Eusebius (about A.D. 320) reports that Papias (about A.D. 130) said that Mark's Gospel was a translation into Greek of the teachings of Peter. He heard Peter preach, and wrote down what he said. It is of interest that Peter's sermon in the home of Cornelius forms a good outline of this Gospel (Acts 10:36ff.). Moule (p. 5) cites a recently discovered letter of Clement of Alexandria (about A.D. 190), which speaks of Peter's notes as forming part of Mark's material. Clearly early Christian tradition links Mark with Peter with respect to this Gospel (cf. I Peter 5:13). So Peter may be regarded as Mark's eye-witness source. Indeed, at least one portion may be seen as auto-biographical (14:51-52).

Most likely this Gospel was the first of the four to be written. Both Matthew and Luke follow its frame-work, though with certain variances.

It was probably written between A.D. 50 and A.D. 55. Some would place it later, after Peter's death perhaps about A.D. 67-68. But the present trend is to date all of the Gospels earlier than a few years ago. In the writer's judgment it should be dated not later than A.D. 55.

This is the final New Testament volume in the Shield Bible Study Series to be published. Earlier it was this writer's privilege to write the one on *The Epistles to the Corinthians* (Baker, 1960). Therefore, it is with gratitude that he has been requested to prepare the material for this volume.

In this study the King James Version has been followed. However, on occasion the writer has supplied his own translations where such seemed desirable to bring out some fine point of meaning. These translations have been from Nestle's *Novum Testamentum Graece.*

Deliberately the writer has used few quotations from other works. This has been done for the sake of brevity. Where used, citations as to sources have been given. For those interested in further study certain standard works are listed:

Robertson, *Word Pictures in the New Testament;* Vol. 1., Sunday School Board of the Southern Baptist Convention, Nashville, 1930; *The Interpreter's Bible,* Vol. VII., "The Gospel According to St. Mark," pp. 629ff.; Abingdon Press, Nashville, 1951; Moule, *The Gospel According to Mark* (Cambridge Bible Commentary, University Press, Cambridge, 1965; Erdman, *The Gospel of Mark,* Westminster Press, Philadelphia, 1966; *The Expositor's Greek Testament,* "Mark," A. B. Bruce, Eerdmans, Grand Rapids, 1951; Morgan, *The Gospel According to Mark,* Revell, Westwood, N. J., 1927; *The International Critical Commentary,* "Mark," Gould, Scribners, New York, 1896; *Broadman Bible Commentary,* "Mark," Turlington, Broadman, Nashville, 1969; *The International Standard Bible Encyclopaedia,* Vol. III., Eerdmans, Grand Rapids, 1949, pp. 1986-1995; Maclaren, *Expositions,* "Mark," Zondervan, Grand Rapids, 1908; Barclay, *The Gospel of Mark,* Westminster, Philadelphia, 1956; Hobbs, *An Exposition of the Gospel of Mark,* Baker, Grand Rapids, 1970; *The Life and Times of Jesus,* Zondervan, Grand Rapids, 1966.

Herschel H. Hobbs

First Baptist Church
Oklahoma City, Oklahoma

OUTLINE OF THE GOSPEL OF MARK

I. THE PREPARATORY PERIOD (1:1-13)

1. The Beginning of the Gospel (1:1-3)
2. The Herald of the King (1:4-8)
3. The Baptism of Jesus ((1:9-11)
4. The Temptation of Jesus (1:12-13)

II. THE GALILEAN MINISTRY (1:14—6:30)

1. The Summary of the Good News (1:14-15)
2. The Call of Four Fishermen (1:16-20)
3. The Healing of a Demon-possessed Man (1:21-28)
4. The Healing of Peter's Mother-in-law (1:29-31)
5. The Growing Popularity (1:32-34)
6. The Quiet Time (1:35-37)
7. The First Tour of Galilee (1:38-39)
8. The Healing of a Leper (1:40-45)
9. The Paralytic Borne of Four (2:1-12)
10. The Call of Levi (2:13-14)
11. The Celebration, Criticism, and Reply (2:15-22)
12. The Sabbath Controversy (2:23—3:6)
13. The Ministry by the Sea (3:7-12)
14. The Choice of the Twelve (3:13-19a)
15. The Zeal of Jesus (3:19b-21)
16. The Unpardonable Sin (3:22-30)
17. The True Relationship (3:31-35)
18. The Parable of the Soils (4:1-20)
19. The Parable of the Lamp (4:21-25)
20. The Parable of Gradual Growth (4:26-29)
21. The Parable of the Mustard Seed (4:30-34)
22. The Storm at Sea (4:35-41)
23. The Healing of a Demoniac (5:1-20)
24. The Daughter of Jairus and the Sick Woman (5:21-43)
25. The Rejection at Nazareth (6:1-6a)
26. The Mission of the Twelve (6:6b-13)
27. The Death of John the Baptist (6:14-29)
28. The Report of the Twelve (6:30)

III. THE PERIOD OF WITHDRAWALS (6:31—9:50)

1. The Feeding of the Five Thousand (6:31-46)
2. The Miracle of Walking on Water (6:47-52)
3. The Ministry at Gennesaret (6:53-56)

4. The Rebuke of the Pharisees (7:1-23)
5. The Syrophoenician Woman (7:24-30)
6. The Healing of a Deaf Mute (7:31-37)
7. The Feeding of the Four Thousand (8:1-9)
8. The Demand for a Sign (8:10-13)
9. The Warning about Leaven (8:14-21)
10. The Healing of the Blind Man (8:22-26)
11. The Examination and Lesson at Caesarea Philippi (8:27—9:1)
12. The Transfiguration of Jesus (9:2-10)
13. The Problem of Elias (9:11-13)
14. The Healing of a Demoniac Boy (9:14-29)
15. The Final Teaching in Galilee (9:30-50)

IV. THE MINISTRY IN PEREA AND JUDEA (10:1-52)

1. The Lesson about Divorce (10:1-12)
2. The Blessing of Children (10:13-16)
3. The Rich Young Ruler (10:17-22)
4. The Peril of Riches (10:23-27)
5. The Matter of Reward (10:28-31)
6. The Prediction of Jesus' Death (10:32-34)
7. The Request for Prominence (10:35-45)
8. The Healing of Bartimaeus (10:46-52)

V. THE EVENTS OF PASSION WEEK (11:1—15:47)

1. The Royal Entry (11:1-11)
2. The Curse of the Barren Fig Tree (11:12-14)
3. The Cleansing of the Temple (11:15-19)
4. The Lesson about Faith (11:20-26)
5. The Challenge to Jesus' Authority (11:27-33)
6. The Parable of the Husbandmen (12:1-12)
7. The Question about Tribute (12:13-17)
8. The Problem of the Resurrection (12:18-27)
9. The Question about the Great Commandment (12:28:34)
10. The Question about the Christ (12:35-37)
11. The Warning against the Scribes (12:38-40)
12. The Widow's Mite (12:41-44)
13. The Eschatalogical Discourse (13:1-37)
14. The Plot of the Sanhedrin (14:1-2)
15. The Dinner in Bethany (14:3-9)
16. The Treachery of Judas (14:10-11)
17. The Passover Meal (14:12-21)
18. The Lord's Supper (14:22-26)
19. The Audacity of Peter (14:27-31)
20. The Prayer Vigil in Gethsemane (14:32-42)
21. The Betrayal and Arrest (14:43-52)

COMMENTARY ON THE GOSPEL OF MARK

I. THE PREPARATORY PERIOD (1:1-13)

1. The Beginning of the Gospel (1:1-3)

"The beginning of the gospel of Jesus Christ" (v. 1). "The Son of God" is not in some strong manuscripts. But it is found in other strong ones. Whether Mark wrote it or it was added later, Mark elsewhere uses the title with respect to Jesus.

"Beginning" in the Greek text is without the definite article. So "a beginning." It could refer to the ministry of John the Baptist. But may also include these various preparatory events. "Gospel" means "good news." It could refer to the good news as such, or it could be the record written by Mark, hence the *Gospel of Mark*. Either makes sense.

"Jesus" is the Greek form of "Joshua" or "Yeshua," meaning Jehovah is salvation. It is the Lord's human, saving name. "Christ" is the Greek equivalent of "Messiah," the anointed one. He was anointed of God to be the Saviour. Mark combines them in one person, the human-divine Son of God as Saviour.

"As it is written in the prophets" (v. 2). The best Greek texts read "In Isaiah, the prophet." Actually, the quotation in verses 2-3 is a combination of Malachi 3:1 (v. 2) and Isaiah 40:3. Mark evidently wrote "in Isaiah, the prophet," and a later scribe corrected it to read "in the prophets." But Isaiah was regarded as the chief of the prophets. Such combinations were commonly used, so actually it was no error on Mark's part by the literary standards of the day. Bruce notes that this is Mark's only prophetic quotation on his own.

The heart of the quotation is in verse 3. It referred to an ancient custom of preparing a smooth road over which a king might ride to visit some part of his realm. God's messenger was sent before the Christ to prepare the way for him to be received into men's hearts.

In the Old Testament context these verses speak of judgment (vs. 2; Mal. 3:1ff.) and *comfort* (v. 3; Isa. 40:1ff.). Christ will judge men in their sins, but will comfort or save those who believe in Him. This is the twofold nature of the "gospel" (cf. Rom. 1:16-18). To preach the gospel one must declare both facets of Christ's work.

2. The Herald of the King (1:4-8)

Writing for the Romans who were interested in action, Mark did not record Jesus' eternal existence, genealogy, or virgin birth. This fact does not militate against any of these (cf. Matt.; Luke; John). He simply plunged into the earthly ministry of Jesus.

"John did baptize in the wilderness, and preach the baptism of repentance for the remission of sins" (v. 4). He made no effort to identify John other than to say, literally, "John came, the one baptizing in the wilderness heralding a baptism of repentance." On John the Baptist see Luke 1:5-23, 57-80.

"Baptize" *(baptizō)* means to dip, submerge, plunge, or immerse. The baptizing took place in the Jordan River which is identified with the deserted region of Judea. "Baptism" *(baptisma)* refers to the meaning in the act. In this case it symbolized "repentance," a change of mind, heart, attitude. "For" renders *eis* which may mean for, unto, into, as the result of, on the basis of, or with respect to. It is translated "at" in Matthew 12:41. In the light of the overall teaching of the New Testament, here it expresses result not purpose. Baptism was the result of the remission of sins.

The Greek word rendered "preach" *(kērussō)* means to herald. A herald of a king was to be heard and obeyed as though he was the king himself.

"All the land of Judaea . . . Jerusalem" (v. 5) does not mean every person. It is hyperbole showing the great crowds. "Were baptized" (imperfect tense) pictures a procession of people submitting to baptism as evidence of "confessing their sins." "In the river Jordan" literally means "in [*en,* in the sphere of] the river."

"Camel's hair" (v. 6) was not a skin but cloth woven out of camel's hair. "Locusts" were dried locusts. "Wild honey" was plentiful, found in the clefts of rocks. Some Bedouins still gather and sell wild honey out of the rocks (Robertson). John reminds one of Elijah, an ascetic withdrawn from society (cf. 9:11-13).

Verses 7-8 give a sample of John's preaching. He magnified the one coming after him as "mightier than I." "Latchet" was a leather thong which held sandals to one's feet. When one arrived as a guest a slave loosed these latchets. John was unworthy to do even this. The coming one was greater in person; and also in work. Unlike John's baptism in water, "He shall baptize you with [in] the Holy Ghost [Spirit]" (v. 8). John's rite was external; Jesus' baptism would effect inner change. John led men to pledge to break with sin; Jesus would cleanse from sin. John was the forerunner of the Christ.

3. The Baptism of Jesus (1:9-11)

"Jesus came from Nazareth of Galilee, and was baptized of John in Jordan." Mark did not explain Jesus' origin, but simply told of His residence. "In Jordan" reads "into *[eis]* the Jordan." They went down *into* the river.

Verse 10 uses the first "straightway" or "immediately" *(euthus).*

"Out of *[ek]* the water." This does not mean coming out of the river itself, but emerging from the baptismal water. In the Greek text "straightway" relates to "he saw." As soon as Jesus came up out of the water He saw the heavens "opened," split like a garment. "And the Spirit like a dove descending upon [*eis*. unto] him." Luke says the Spirit was in the shape of a dove (3:22), suggesting the totality of the Spirit. He came upon Jesus in fulness, anointing Him for His work. Jesus never performed a miracle until after this anointing with power. He was divine, but also human. So He needed this anointing power.

"And there came a voice from [*ek,* out of] heaven, saying, "Thou art my beloved Son, in whom I am well pleased" (v. 11). "Thou" is written out, so emphatic. "Thou and no one else." Jesus was/is the unique Son of God. Note the threefold presence of deity: Father (voice), Son (Jesus), Holy Spirit (dove). The triune God evidenced as Jesus began His public ministry.

Why was Jesus baptized? Not in confession of sin, for He had none. Perhaps three things explain it. Jesus authenticated John's ministry. He identified Himself with sinful men. He officially began His ministry.

In His baptism there is a prophecy of His death and resurrection. Also the dove was symbolic of innocence and sacrifice. So there is suggested the sacrifice of the sinless one. God's voice authenticated Jesus as God's approved Son (cf. 9:7).

Both John and Jesus saw the *dove* and heard the voice. The Spirit descending upon Jesus was John's sign from God as to the identity of the Messiah (cf. John 1:33). So this baptism marked the climax of John's ministry and the beginning of that of Jesus.

4. The Temptation of Jesus (1:12-13)

"And immediately [*euthus*] the Spirit driveth him into the wilderness" (v. 12). "Driveth" is peculiar to Mark (cf. Matt. 4:1, "led up"; Luke 4:1, "led"). The Holy Spirit was with Jesus throughout this experience. "Wilderness" was the barren Judean hills west of Jericho. Tradition says that it was on Quarantania, a mountain just west of Jericho. This name comes from "forty days" (v. 13).

"Wild beasts" (v. 13). The area was full of wild animals: wolf, boar, hyena, jackal, leopard (Robertson). Only Mark mentions this. Jesus was exposed to danger, hunger, and loneliness. "Tempted" renders *peirazō,* to test or tempt. It means to test or try in order to prove something genuine or false. What kind of Messiah would Jesus be? Would He follow God's will or Satan's? See Matthew 4 and Luke 4 for details. Jesus followed God's will and rejected that of Satan. So He was genuine. "Angels ministered unto him." "Ministered" is an imperfect tense. They did so repeatedly until Jesus was cheered and strengthened (Robertson).

II. THE GALILEAN MINISTRY (1:14–6:30)

Mark omitted the account of the opening months of Jesus' ministry recorded in John 1:35—4:43, and is followed by Matthew and Luke. John records very little of the Galilean ministry, but shows knowledge of it (4:43ff.; 6). Mark's account, however, fits into John's record. This fact is seen in his note that Jesus returned to Galilee after John the Baptist's imprisonment (cf. John 4:1-4).

1. The Summary of the Good News (1:14-15)

Jesus came into Galilee "preaching the gospel [good news] of the kingdom of God" (v. 14). The best texts read "the gospel of God." In essence He heralded the same message as that of John. This is clearly seen in verse 15.

"The time is fulfilled." God's promise of the Messiah has been brought to fruition. Note Paul's "fulness of the time" (Gal. 4:4; cf. Eph. 1:10). "Time" is *kairos,* meaning opportunity or crisis. It was indeed a crisis-opportunity for mankind. "The kingdom is at hand." The kingdom came with the King. So Jesus called for repentance and faith in the gospel.

"Repent" means to change one's mind, heart, attitude. It connotes a complete change. The verb *metanoeō* is composed of *meta,* about, and *noeō* from *nous,* mind, referring to the entire person. "Believe" means to believe, trust, commit. It involves both intellect and volition. Believe the gospel, trust in it, and commit one's way to it. Of course, Christ is central in the gospel. So Jesus called for repentance toward God and faith in Himself.

2. The Call of Four Fishermen (1:16-20)

From this summary statement Mark moved quickly to record specific events.

Literally, "And passing along by the sea of Galilee, he saw Simon and Andrew, the brother of Simon, casting on both sides in the sea" (v. 16). This is the first mention of these two brothers. Simon was evidently known to Mark's readers. He identified Andrew as his brother (cf. John 1:40). "Brother" *(adelphos)* comes from *adelphus,* meaning from the same womb. "Net" does not appear in the Greek text, but is understood from "casting" (*amphiballontes,* casting on both sides, of the boat). "For they were fishers."

"Come ye after me, and I will make you to become fishers of men" (v. 17). Note the future "I will make." "Become" means to become something they had not been previously. From fishers after fish they will become fishers after men. "And straightway *[euthus]* they forsook their nets, and followed him" (v. 18). To follow means to go along with one, sharing his experiences of hardship and joy. They did this for Jesus.

Farther along the shore Jesus saw James and John, sons of Zebedee, "mending their nets" (v. 19). This was necessary after a night of fishing. One still sees this scene along the sea of Galilee. Luke says that these two pairs of brothers were partners (5:7). Jesus issued the same call to James and John. With the same result (v. 20). They left their father in the ship with "the hired servants" (*misthōtōn,* not slaves, they worked for wages).

John tells of the previous experience of Simon, Andrew, John (implied), and probably James with Jesus (1:37-42). This explains their present readiness to follow Him. Jesus still calls men to leave their economic vocations to follow and serve Him in special ways. But He calls all Christians to follow and serve Him.

3. The Healing of a Demon-possessed Man (1:21-28)

This is Mark's first account of a miracle by Jesus. But see John (2:1ff., 23; 3:2; 4:46ff.). Mark's Roman readers would be interested in miracles. So Mark placed great emphasis upon such (cf. 2:23–3:30).

This first recorded miracle in Mark showed Jesus' power over demons. Early in Jesus' Galilean ministry He established headquarters in Capernaum, on the north shore of the sea of Galilee. "And straightway on the sabbath day he entered into the synogogue, and taught" (v. 21). The remains of a later synagogue probably built on the site of this one may be seen today. Robertson calls "taught" (*edidasken*) an inchoative imperfect. He "began to teach" as soon as He entered the synagogue. Note that it was on the Sabbath Day.

"Astonished" means to strike a person out of his senses by some strong feeling such as joy, fear, or wonder. The imperfect tense means that as Jesus was teaching they were astonished. "At his doctrine" or "teaching." He taught not by rote words quoted from others as did the Jewish scribes. His teaching was as one who had "authority." This renders *exousian,* out of being. Jesus taught out of the very nature of His being.

"A man with [*en,* in the sphere of] an unclean spirit" (v. 23). The demon was in the man and the man was in the demon. The demon cried out, "What to us and to you?" (v. 24). Note the plural "us," the demon and the demon-possessed man. What did they have in common with Jesus? The demon addressed "Jesus of Nazareth" as one come to destroy them. Jesus came to destroy the work of Satan but to save men. "I know thee who thou art, the Holy One of God" (v. 24). The demon speaking. "Know" *(oida)* means to know fully by perception. Though men may not have recognized Jesus, demons did. Jesus rebuked the demon. "Hold thy peace [be muzzled like an ox], and come out of him" (v. 25). Jesus did not want the confession of demons. Soon enough His enemies would accuse Him of being in league with Satan (cf. 3:22). The demon obeyed (v. 26). But as it did so it *tore* the man, threw him into a spasm. He also "cried with a loud voice," a screech. A dramatic and exciting event!

The people were amazed (v. 27). They "questioned among themselves." Literally, "they sought together" an answer. They had heard "a new [fresh] doctrine" or "teaching." And Jesus also worked with "authority" (*exousian,* out of being). Jesus both taught and worked with power out of Himself (cf. v. 22).

No wonder that Jesus' "fame" (report or rumor) spread throughout Galilee and surrounding areas (v. 28). The rumor mills were busy.

4. The Healing of Peter's Mother-in-law (1:29-31)

This miracle shows Jesus' power over disease. After *church* Jesus went home with Simon and Andrew, accompanied by James and John (v. 29). Perhaps Jesus lived here while in Capernaum. Peter's wife's mother "lay sick of a fever" (v. 30). She "lay prostrate burning with fever." Luke used the medical phrase "holden with a great fever."

Hearing of it Jesus seized her hand and lifted her up. "And immediately the fever left her, and she ministered unto them" (v. 31). It was a miracle as shown by the immediate leaving (aorist tense) of the fever, and that she "went on serving them" with full bodily strength. An ordinary healing and strengthening would have been gradual. Did she serve the Sabbath meal?

5. The Growing Popularity (1:32-34)

This records many healings. "And at even, when the sun did set" (v. 32). People were forbidden by the scribes to carry their sick on the Sabbath. It ended at sunset. So "they brought" in a steady stream (imperfect) their sick and demonized. So that "all the city was gathered at the door" (v. 33).

So Jesus healed them. Note again that He forbade demons to speak of Him (v. 34). It was a beautiful ending to this Sabbath Day. From this time on the Galilean crowds flocked to Jesus. But they left Him when He refused to become a Bread-Political-Military Messiah (cf. John 6).

6. The Quiet Time (1:35-37)

The previous day had exhausted Jesus physically and emotionally. So "in the morning, rising up a great while before day, he went out, and departed into a solitary place, and there prayed" (v. 35). "In the morning" renders *prōi,* the last watch of the night, 3:00-6:00 A.M. "A great while before day" *(ennucha lian),* the early part of the *proī,* still dark. "Rising up" from bed, and "went out." out of both the house and city. And He "was praying" (imperfect). If Jesus needed this quiet hour, how much more so do others!

"And Simon and they that were with him followed after him" (v. 36). "Followed after" (*katediōxen*) means that they hunted until they found him.

"All men seek thee" (v. 37). They thought that this would surely bring Jesus back to the crowds. But they were in for a surprise.

7. The First Tour of Galilee (1:38-39)

Rather than to follow the lure of the crowd Jesus said, "Let us go into the next towns, that I may preach there also: for therefore came I forth" (v. 38). Jesus proposed to leave the city crowds to preach in smaller places. The need was there also. "For therefore came I forth" could mean the purpose of Jesus' incarnation. But more likely He meant that He left Capernaum for this purpose. He knew about the crowds, but He also knew of the need elsewhere. All men must have an opportunity to hear Him herald the gospel of God (cf. 1:15).

He *came preaching* "in their synagogues throughout all Galilee, and cast out devils" (v. 39).

8. The Healing of a Leper (1:40-45)

During this tour Jesus healed a leper, showing His power over this dreaded disease. Luke says that this took pláce in a city (5:12). Palestine had two types of leprosy: a skin disease, and one beginning with a small spot which spread and grew progressively worse. It ate away the flesh until only stumps of hands or legs were left. It was a living death lasting for years. Luke says that this man was full of leprosy, so probably in its last stages.

Lepers were isolated from people, forbidden to enter walled cities. Strangely in the final stage they were permitted in cities. This explains why this one was in a city.

"If thou wilt, thou canst make me clean" (v. 40). He did not question Jesus' power but His will to do this. But note His response. He "touched him" (v. 41). Such was unheard of. One rabbi boasted of throwing rocks at a leper to drive him away. But Jesus *touched an untouchable*. He said, "I will [am willing]; be thou clean." He had both the will and the power to heal. "Left" and "was cleansed" are aorist tenses (v. 42). These plus "immediately" *(euthus)* show the miraculous cure.

"And he straitly charged him, and forthwith sent him away" (v. 43). "Straitly charged" renders a verb expressing strong emotion. Here a stern admonition to tell no one about it (v. 44a). Evidently those present knew about the cure. But Jesus did not want the word scattered abroad and thus create undue excitement. He did not wish to be known merely as a wonder-worker.

Note that while Jesus healed miraculously, He did not ignore the Mosaic law for cleansed lepers. He told him to go to a priest and make the required offering, so that the priest could give "testimony" (witness) to people that he was officially clean (v. 44). Only thus could the man be received back into society.

However, the man went out and "began to publish it much" (v. 45).

"To publish" renders *kērussein,* to preach. He did it so much that Jesus was forced to avoid thickly populated areas. However, people "kept coming" (imperfect) from all over. One of Jesus' problems was to get the Galileans to see Him as other than a miracle man. These external *signs* of His deity were largely lost on them.

9. The Paralytic Borne of Four (2:1-12)

"After some days" describes the time of Jesus' tour of Galilee (v. 1). Back in Capernaum "it was noised [heard] that he was in the house." Perhaps Peter's house. "Many were gathered together." The aorist tense shows how quickly they came. They filled the house and massed about the door. Literally, "And he was speaking to them the word" (v. 2).

Four men brought to Jesus "one sick of the palsy" or a paralytic (*paralutikon,* v. 3). He was on a pallet or poor man's bed with one bearer at each corner. "Press" means "crowd" (v. 4). Unable to enter the door "they uncovered the roof" or "unroofed the roof." They probably took him to the flat roof by way of outside stairs. Probably by ropes fastened to each corner of the bed they lowered the paralytic into Jesus' presence.

"When Jesus saw their faith [the four men and the paralytic], he said unto the paralytic, Son, thy sins be forgiven thee" (v. 5). Note that He forgave the man's sins rather than to heal him. Were his sins responsible for his condition? Jesus did the more important thing first.

"Certain . . . scribes sitting there and reasoning in their hearts" (v. 6). They were there to find fault with Jesus. His popularity alarmed them. They did not speak aloud. But buzzing among themselves, Jesus knew their thoughts.

They accused Jesus of blasphemy. "Who can forgive sins but God only?" (v. 7). To blaspheme means to speak slanderously. They accused Jesus of such as He assumed this divine prerogative. True, only God can forgive sins.

Jesus took them at their word (v. 8). "Whether it be easier to say . . . Thy sins be forgiven thee; or to say, Arise, and take up thy bed, and walk?" (v. 9); or "go on walking about." Obviously the former was easier, for no one could check on the result. The latter would be a visible sign. So Jesus performed the physical miracle as proof of the former power.

"Know" (v. 10) means to have perceptive knowledge. No question about it. "Power" is *exousian,* power or authority out of Jesus' very nature or being. Power to heal would prove His power to forgive. Note "Son of man," Christ's favorite title for Himself; identified with man, but also a Messianic title.

"Arise and take up thy bed, and go thy way into thine house" (v. 11). The man responded immediately as seen in the aorist verbs plus "immediately" (*euthus,* v. 12). "Went forth before them all," before their faces (*emprosthen*). The amazed people said, "We never saw it on this fashion" (v. 12). "Never at any time" *(oudepote)*. Jesus had proved His power in both cases. Those who saw it could not deny it, not even the scribes. The people were "amazed" or in an ecstasy *(existastai)* and glorified God. The scribes *saw*, but refused to accept the evidence.

10. The Call of Levi (2:13-14)

From the house Jesus "went forth" to walk "by [*para*, alongside] the sea" (v. 13). When one walks by the sea of Galilee, he truly walks where Jesus walked. This was probably to get a breath of fresh air away from the crowd. But they "resorted [were coming, imperfect] unto him, and he taught [was teaching, imperfect] them." These tenses make the scene live.

Passing along "he saw Levi the son of Alphaeus sitting at the receipt of custom" (v. 14). Levi was also called Matthew (Matt. 9:9). The "seat of custom" was the tollgate *(telōnion)* on the road from Damascus to the Mediterranean. Levi was a publican *(telōnēs)* serving under Herod Antipas who ruled under the Romans as a tetrarch over Galilee and Perea. The Jews despised publicans as traitors to their people. They were classed with sinners, "publicans and sinners" (v. 16). Such was an unlikely follower of Jesus. But Jesus saw qualities in him which led Him later to choose him as one of the twelve apostles (cf. 3:18).

So Jesus said, "Follow me" (v. 14; cf. 1:17, 20). Whether Levi had previously believed in Jesus is not stated. Probably so. In any event he immediately "arose" and "followed" Him. He left the tax table to serve the Lord.

11. The Celebration, Criticism, and Reply (2:15-22)

This was a great day in Levi's life. So he gave a dinner to celebrate it (v. 15). Reclining at the table were Jesus, His disciples, "and many publicans and sinners." Levi invited his friends to the dinner. They too "followed" Jesus. Levi's witness bore fruit among his friends.

It was customary for outsiders to stand about and watch as guests ate. Among them were "scribes and Pharisees" or, literally, "scribes of the Pharisees" (v. 16). They came to criticize. So they asked Jesus' disciples, "How is it that he eateth . . . with publicans and sinners?" (v. 16). "And drinketh" is not in the best texts. This question implied that Jesus was one of them, agreed with and possibly shared in their misdeeds.

Hearing their question Jesus replied, "They that are whole have no need of a physician, but they that are sick" (v. 17). The scribes regarded publicans and sinners as morally ill, and themselves as well. So Jesus took them at their word. The *sick* needed Him; the *well* did not. Where would one expect to find a physician? Among the sick. Applying it Jesus said, "I came not to call the righteous, but sinners" (v. 17).

"To repentance" is not genuine in Mark but is genuine in Luke 5:32.

Answered at this point the critics made another try. Literally, "the disciples of John and the Pharisees were fasting" (v. 18). It may have been one of the Jewish fast days (second and fifth days of the week for stricter Jews, Robertson). Apparently the disciples of John also were observing this fast day. Their leader was in prison. But Jesus and His disciples were feasting. Hence their criticism. But John's disciples had missed the point of their teacher's loyalty to Jesus.

"Can the children [sons] of the bridechamber fast, while the bridegroom is with them?" (v. 19). John had called Jesus the "bridegroom" (John 3:29). So Jesus answered John's disciples with their teacher's own words. A wedding feast is a time for feasting, not fasting. So long as Jesus was with His disciples "it is not possible to fast." When Jesus is taken from them in His crucifixion, they will fast (v. 20). But not for long. The resurrection will turn sadness into joy.

Then Jesus applied His words. "No man also seweth a piece of new cloth on an old garment; else the new piece that filled it up taketh away from the old, and the new rent is made worse" (v. 21). New unshrunk cloth would shrink and tear a larger hole in the old cloth. In essence, Jesus came not to patch up an old worn out Judaism, but to provide the new cloth of Christian freedom.

"And no man putteth new wine into old bottles [wineskins]: else the new wine doth burst the bottles [wineskins], and the wine is spilled, and the bottles [wineskins] will be marred [destroyed]: but new wine must be put into new [*kainous,* fresh] bottles [wineskins]" (v. 22).

Old wineskins became dry and brittle. New wine continued to ferment producing gases. As the old skins stretched they burst, spilling the wine. New skins were elastic, so they expanded so as to accommodate the gas and contain the wine.

In essence, the disciples of John and the Pharisees were trying to pour new truth into the old legalistic forms of Judaism. Such was impossible. The new revelation in Christ must be contained in new forms. Much error has entered Christianity as its truth is related to old legal forms of the Old Testament. To attempt to do so is to lose the essence of the truth and freedom provided in Christ.

12. The Sabbath Controversy (2:23–3:6)

This event took place following Jesus' visit to Jerusalem recorded in John 5. While Jesus was there He healed the lame man at the pool of Bethesda. It was on the Sabbath. For the first time the Jewish rulers attacked Jesus for disregarding their Sabbath rules against any type of work, even healing. Though He had healed on the Sabbath in Galilee, this was the first in Jerusalem. So the rulers had an issue, and they played it to the hilt.

Judaism had four cardinal things: Scriptures, temple, traditions, and the Sabbath. Only the last was peculiar to Judaism among the world's religions. So the Jews were very sensitive at this point.

They had hundreds of ridiculous rules governing conduct on the Sabbath. Any *work* was forbidden. Appropriate to this passage were the following: to pull a head of grain was *reaping;* to rub out the grain in one's hand was *threshing.*

On their way back to Galilee on a Sabbath Day Jesus and His disciples passed through a grain field (v. 23). Foot paths were provided for this purpose. "As they went, to pluck ears of corn" or "heads of grain." It was permissible to do this to get food so long as they did not reap the grain. Implied is that they rubbed out the grain in their hands, and ate it. These were *reaping* and *threshing.*

"Behold, why do they on the sabbath day that which is not lawful?" (v. 24). It was permitted by Moses' law (Lev. 23:25), but forbidden by the scribes' law. However, Jesus justified the practice by referring to an instance from Scripture: necessity (vv. 25f.; cf. I Sam. 21:1-6). Man's needs came before an institution. Then Jesus applied the lesson.

"The sabbath was made for man, and not man for the sabbath" (v. 27). It was for man's blessing, not as a burden to be borne. This does not mean a wide-open Sunday. The Sabbath should be used for rest and worship, to strengthen both body and spirit.

"Therefore the Son of man is Lord also of the sabbath" (v. 28). This was a tremendous claim. Jesus had shown His Lordship over the temple (John 2:13ff.). He will show His Lordship over the Scriptures (Matt. 5:17ff.) and tradition (Mark 7:1ff.). And here, over the Sabbath. He is Lord over all. He never broke one of God's laws, but He brushed aside the man-made rules which were a burden to man. As to the Sabbath He placed it in the right perspective in God's plan.

Back in Capernaum Jesus was in the synagogue on the Sabbath Day. "And there was a man which had a withered hand" (3:1). Luke notes that it was his right hand, his working hand (6:6). It was so by accident or disease, not congenital (Robertson).

"And they watched him, whether he would heal him on the sabbath day; that they might accuse him" (v. 2). These were the Pharisees. "Watched" means that they were "watching on the sly" (imperfect). Wycliff says, "They aspied in him." Would Jesus violate their Sabbath rules again?

"Stand forth" (v. 3). Literally, "rise into the middle," the middle of the room. Jesus wanted all to see him. He defied the spies. "Is is lawful to do good on the sabbath days . . . or evil? to save life, or to kill?" (v. 4). To say "yes" to "do good" and "save life" would have denied their Sabbath rules. Obviously they could not condone "evil . . . kill." So they "kept on holding their peace." To them silence was the safest thing. Jesus exposed their hypocrisy.

With indignant anger Jesus looked about the room. "Stretch forth thine hand" (v. 5), for all to see. And the withered hand was restored immediately as good as the other one. A miracle for all to see.

But it did not convince the hard hearts of the Pharisees. Immediately they left the synagogue, "and took counsel with the Herodians against him, how they might destroy him" (v. 6). This was a strange coalition: Pharisees and Herodians. The former were committed to restoring the Jewish kingdom; the latter were champions of the Herodian family to rule. So they were bitter enemies. But their common hatred for Jesus made strange bedfellows.

13. The Ministry by the Sea (3:7-12)

Jesus and His disciples left the synagogue to walk along the sea of Galilee. But the crowds followed them. Jesus' fame had spread as shown by the places mentioned in verses 7-8. The synagogue could no longer contain the people.

So Jesus instructed the disciples to prepare a small boat, "lest they should throng him" (v. 9) or "crush" *(thlibōsin,* like crushing grapes in a press). Here Jesus healed many of diseases (v. 10). While not stated it is implied that He cast out demons. For they, perhaps the demonized, "kept falling down" before Him, and "kept crying, saying, Thou art the Son of God" (v. 11). Jesus "kept rebuking" them that they should not make Him known (v. 12). The imperfect tenses make this scene live. As before, Jesus did not want the witness of demons.

14. The Choice of the Twelve (3:13-19a)

According to Robertson's *A Harmony of the Gospels* this event took place just before the Sermon on the Mount (cf. Luke 6:12-16). It was about half-way through Jesus' public ministry.

After a night of prayer He chose the twelve apostles (cf. Luke 6:12ff.). He called to Himself "whom he would" (v. 13). The Greek is emphatic, "whom he himself would" or "wished," "willed." "And they came [went off] unto him." They became an inner circle apart from the greater body of disciples.

"And he ordained [made] twelve" (v. 14). Mark lists three reasons for this choice (vv. 14-15). (1) That they should be with Him for special training. (2) That He might send them forth to preach. (3) That they might have power to heal sicknesses and cast out demons. Note that "send forth" *(apostellēi)* is the verb akin to *apostles,* sent forth ones.

The apostles are listed in verses 16-19 (cf. Matt. 10:2f.; Luke 6:14f.; Acts 1:13f). Note that Peter always comes first, followed by James, John, Andrew, and Philip. Also note that Peter, Philip, and James the son of Alpheus head groups of three. Peter, James, and John formed a special group or inner circle. Peter heading the list does not mean that he was the chief apostle. Usually he spoke for the group out of impetuosity. But Jesus was the Head of the Twelve.

There are three sets of brothers: Peter and Andrew; James and John; James the son of Alpheus and Judas the brother of James.

Judas Iscariot always appears last. In Acts he is not listed, since he was already dead.

This was a complex group indeed. But Jesus molded them into a unit. Perhaps each had qualities which Jesus would use in His kingdom. Only Judas failed to give himself to Jesus.

15. The Zeal of Jesus (3:19b-21)

Mark did not record the Sermon on the Mount. The Roman readers were not interested in Jesus' teachings, only in His works.

The Greek text reads, "And he comes into a house" (v. 19b.; but v. 20 in Greek text). The crowds also came together, "so that they could not so much as eat bread" (v. 20). This included all, even Jesus. They did not take time out to eat. Jesus was so absorbed in ministering that He doubtless lost all sense of physical need.

"Friends... went out to lay hold on him" (v. 21). "His friends," literally, "the ones alongside him." Some relate these to Jesus' mother and half-brothers (v. 31). But there is no valid reason for this, even though the Septuagint did use this phrase in this manner. The two events are separate in Mark. These were probably disciples other than the Twelve.

"He is beside himself" (v. 21). Or "He stands outside himself." They took Jesus' zeal to be madness. Such is often the case when one has unusual zeal for Christ. But in their case, as in His, it is a holy zeal for the things of God.

16. The Unpardonable Sin (3:22-30)

Matthew sets this in the context of the healing of a demoniac (12:22f.). The people saw it, and recognized Jesus as the Christ.

But the scribes sent from Jerusalem to oppose Jesus said, "He hath Beelzebub, and by the prince of devils casteth he out devils" or demons (v. 22). The Greek reads "Beelzebul," probably formed on Baal, the Canaanite god of fertility (cf. Beel-Zebub, the fly god of Ekron, II Kings 1:2-3, 6, 16). He was probably called the fly god since flies abounded in Palestine during the growing season, the time of his ascendency. Jews in contempt applied this name to Satan. So the scribes accused Jesus of being in league with Satan and working by his power. They could not deny the miracle. so they falsified as to the source of power.

Jesus refuted their charge (vv. 23-27). "How can Satan cast out Satan?" (v. 23). His would be a divided kingdom or house which would be self-destructive (vv. 24-26). This shows how ridiculous was their charge. Conversely, Jesus' work showed that He was more powerful than Satan (v. 27).

Then He drew a conclusion. "Verily" introduces a solemn statement. "All sins" and "blasphemies" shall be forgiven, save one (v. 28). "But he that shall blaspheme against the Holy Ghost [Spirit] hath never forgiveness, but is in danger of eternal damnation: because they said, He hath an unclean spirit" (vv. 29-30). "Blaspheme" *(blasphēmeō)* means to speak slanderously, insultingly against one so as to defame his character. Jesus had worked obviously by the *Holy* Spirit. The scribes said it was by an *evil* spirit. An evident good work, yet they saw it as evil. Their gradual but adamant opposition to Jesus had resulted in their loss of ability to discern between good and evil. To them evil had become good, and good evil.

Literally Jesus said, "They keep on not having forgiveness unto the ages, but are guilty of an eternal sin." Rejecting the Holy Spirit they rejected deity. No Holy Spirit, no conviction. No conviction, no repentance. No repentance, no faith. No faith, no salvation. An eternal sin.

Can one commit this sin today? Some say "no," since to them Jesus must be on earth doing His work. But He is here in His Spirit. This sin is not a sin of the flesh but of the spirit. It is not one of ignorance or impulse, but is one of full-knowledge of Jesus and is deliberate. One who has no sense of sin or need for a Saviour should beware. If one thinks he has committed this sin, he has not. For he is still being convicted by the Holy Spirit. The Christian cannot commit it. He is already saved and sealed unto God by the Holy Spirit (cf. Eph. 1:13-14).

17. The True Relationship (3:31-35)

At this point Jesus' mother and half-brothers came to see Him (v. 31). "Behold, thy mother and thy brethren without seek thee" (v. 32). "Without" or outside the house. For "brethren" see Mark 6:3 (cf. Matt. 13:55).

Already it has been noted that there is no real reason for relating them to "friends" in 3:21. They could have come simply for a visit.

"Who is my mother, or my brethren?" (v. 33). Not just a genetical but a spiritual relationship as is shown in verses 34-35. Genetically Jesus was Mary's Son and a half-brother to her other sons. But actually He was God's Son and their Saviour through faith in Him. God's will was that they and all men receive Him as such.

18. The Parable of the Soils (4:1-25)

On one occasion the crowds were so great that, in order for all to see and hear, Jesus sat in a boat just off the shore of the sea of Galilee (v. 1). "And he taught them many things in parables" (v. 2). "Taught" is an imperfect tense expressing a lengthy teaching. "Doctrine" is the noun form, "teaching." "Parable" renders *parabolais,* meaning casting alongside. It was a favorite method of Jesus' teaching. But here He used a group of parables (cf. v. 34). In Matthew's account (13:3-53) there are eight parables. But Mark only records four (Soils, Lamp, Seed, Mustard Seed).

In a parable one taught spiritual truth from a life situation. The life situation was cast alongside a spiritual truth. Someone defined a parable as an earthly story with a heavenly meaning. Another as a handle by which to bear spiritual truth.

"There went out a sower to sow" (v. 3). It was a common sight in Palestine. It is even possible that someone was sowing seed nearby. Hence the figure. Usually sowing was done by broadcasting the seed so that it fell on different types of soil.

Some fell "by the way side" (v. 4), perhaps on a footpath through the field. It was eaten by birds. Others fell "on stony ground" (v. 5). Much of Palestine is underlaid by limestone rock with a thin covering of soil. "Immediately it sprang up." Thin soil plus warmth in the rock would cause it to sprout and grow quickly in the spring. But with shallow soil it had no firm roots. When the hot sun hit it it soon withered and died. So no yield.

Some seed "fell among thorns" (v. 7). In plowed soil there might be thorn roots which grew rapidly, taking from the seed needed moisture and nurture. The wheat was "choked" or strangled by the thorns. "Yielded no fruit" or barren as to results.

Other fell on "good ground" (v. 8). Good soil with no thorns. It flourished and brought forth "some thirty, and some sixty, and some an hundred" (v. 8). Quite a harvest, but such has been known in the Middle East. Verse 9 was simply urging Jesus' listeners to take heed to what He said. Note the same kind of seed fell on different soils with different results. Hence the parable of the *soils*.

But the Twelve did not understand the parable. So privately they asked Jesus to explain it (v. 10). He replied that the parable was intended to reveal to his friends the mystery of the kingdom of God. But it was designed to conceal this truth from those opposed to Him (v. 11). Then He cited Isaiah 6:9-10. This is a difficult passage to interpret.

"Perceive" means really to know. "Understand" means to comprehend truth. So parables were heard by unbelievers, but they did not really get the meaning of them. Like the scribes and Pharisees they would only use the facts as a basis of opposition to Jesus. "Lest . . . them" sounds like God does not want them to change. This is contrary to His nature. The point is that this failure to comprehend the parables is the result of wilful blindness. They refused to know and understand, so God permitted their refusal to bear its own fruit. Then Jesus proceeded to explain the parable to the disciples (v. 13).,

The seed is "the word" or the gospel (v. 14). "By the way side" are the hard hearted (v. 15). Satan takes away the word before it germinates. "Stony ground" is superficial hearers (v. 16). No real spiritual experience. With "no root in themselves" they soon wilt under persecution (v. 17). "Among thorns" actually hear and receive the word

(v. 18). It begins to grow. But "the cares of the world [Christians divided between God's will and worldly things], deceitfulness of riches, and the lusts of other things" choke out the *wheat* so that it bears no fruit. Unfruitful Christians (v. 19). "Good ground" is those who receive the word, are dedicated to God's will alone. So they bear an abundant harvest (v. 20).

The same gospel is preached to all. The "sower" (v. 14) is anyone who witnesses to it. The fruit borne is determined by the type of *soil* in the lives of the hearers. Seen from the standpoint of the "sower," he is responsible for sowing the word, but not for results. From the viewpoint of the *soils,* each hearer is responsible to God for the fruit or lack of it.

19. The Parable of the Lamp (4:21-25)

The point of this parable is that truth is to be revealed and not concealed. "Candle" *(luchnos)* is "lamp" (v. 21). To light a home one does not put the lamp under a grain measure or bed. It is put on the *lampstand* (candlestick) so as to give light throughout the room. Truth is to be revealed and not hidden (v. 22). Verse 23 repeats verse 9.

One should be careful how and what he hears (v. 24). Careful attention will result in more knowledge. But one who refuses to hear will lose what he thinks he knows (v. 25). The preacher or teacher is responsible for proper preparation and delivery. But the listener is also responsible for proper hearing and use of what he hears.

20. The Parable of Gradual Growth (4:26-29)

The lesson of this parable is that of gradual growth and fruitage of the word of God. The "kingdom of God" grows quietly, but it does grow (v. 26). "Cast seed into the ground." A common sight.

Having done so the sower goes about his business – sleeping and rising night and day (v. 27). All the while by God's power the seed comes up and grows. "He knoweth *[oidate]* not how." He knows by experience *[ginoskō]* that it happens. But he does not really understand *(oidate)* it.

For the earth bringeth forth fruit of herself [*automatē,* automatically]; first the blade, then the ear, after that the full corn in the ear" (v. 28). Man sows God's seed in the soul. It grows and bears fruit, not by man's effort, but by God's power. It does so quietly but surely. Jesus had faith to believe that the kingdom would succeed. Christians should sow faithfully, and leave the results with the Lord. God will surely reap His harvest when it is ready (v. 29).

21. The Parable of the Mustard Seed (4:30-34)

The lesson here is that from small beginnings the kingdom shall reach great proportions. "The kingdom of God . . . like a grain of mustard seed" (vv. 30f.). "Less than all the seeds" is hyperbole, but it means a very small beginning. Such "keeps on growing up, and becometh greater than all herbs" (v. 32). It becomes a tree "so that fowls of the air may lodge under the shadow of it."

Some see "fowls" as symbolic of evil which will enter into the earthly kingdom. But this evidently was not Jesus' thought. He was simply showing how under God's power a small beginning reaches such great proportions.

"Many parables" may be seen in Matthew's account. Mark notes but did not record them all. The truths of the kingdom were hidden from Jesus' enemies, but he disclosed their meaning to His disciples (vv. 33f.)

22. The Storm at Sea (4:35-41)

Robertson calls this day Jesus' "Busy Day." Late in the afternoon He told His disciples that they would cross the sea of Galilee to the eastern side (v. 35). He wanted to rest. The crowd was dismissed, and they embarked in a boat. But some of the crowd followed in little boats (v. 36).

"And there arose a great storm of wind" (v. 37). Mark says *"a lailaps,"* cyclonic gusts. But Matthew called it a *seismos*. The sea heaved and tossed as an earthquake. Such was/are common as the wind rushes down from Mt. Hermon. The hot air at the sea level (682 feet below sea level) draws the wind down with great force. Evidently the other boats turned back.

"The waves beat [kept beating, imperfect] into the ship, so that it was now full [now filling]" with water (v. 37). It is a vivid picture of a small fishing boat being overrun by giant waves. One can see the disciples rowing and bailing out the water.

All the while Jesus was in the rear of the boat, "asleep on a pillow" (v. 38). The pillow or cushion was on the steermaster's seat. Note the eye-witness detail, evidently supplied by Peter. The disciples were frantic, but Jesus was calmly sleeping. It was a sleep of physical exhaustion and spiritual faith.

Some of the disciples were experts at sailing boats. But when they had done their best only to fail, they awoke Jesus. "Master, carest thou not that we perish?" or "are being destroyed?" (v. 38). They rebuked Jesus for sleeping in a storm. But it was also a cry for help. Luke 8:24 uses instead of "Master," teacher, *epistata* (twice), the word for a sea captain.

Jesus arose and "rebuked the wind" (v. 39). "Peace, be still." Note that He spoke to the sea as He would to a person. It was His sea. "And the wind ceased [aorist, immediate ceasing, a miracle], and there was [*egeneto,* became, aorist] a great calm" (v. 39). The sea calmed at once, not gradually. It was a miracle indeed.

"Why are ye so fearful? how is it that ye have no faith?" (v. 40) Jesus rebuked the Twelve for lack of faith. Did they not know that

God would not allow Him to die in a storm? He was still Master even if asleep in a storm. The Twelve had accepted His Messiahship. But, at yet, they did not fully understand it.

"They feared exceedingly." Or "they feared a great fear." Literally, "Who then is this, that even the wind and the sea obey him?" (v. 41). To them this was a greater miracle than those related to healing. He was also Master over the powerful forces of nature!

23. The Healing of a Demoniac (5:1-20)

Soon they were on the eastern shore "into the country [region] of the Gadarenes" (v. 1). The best texts read "Gerasenes" (cf. Luke 8:26; but Matt. 8:28 reads "Gadarenes"). The village of Gerasa was in the district of Gadara. So all three Gospels are correct.

"Out of the tombs a man with an unclean spirit" (v. 2). As such he was driven out of society and lived in the tombs. "No man could bind him, no, not with chains" or a chain (v. 3). This is further explained in verse 4. He was a maniac possessing great strength. No wonder that he could not live among people! Night and day people heard his loud screeches. In his frenzy he cut himself with stones (v. 5). It is a pitiful sight.

Seeing Jesus from afar, he "ran and worshipped" Him (v. 6). Actually, he probably ran toward Jesus in a rage. But when he came into His presence he fell on his knees before Him. This running toward them must have frightened the Twelve. Perhaps Jesus' lack of fear and His very spiritual power caused the man to fall before Him.

The demon cried out through its victim. Literally, "What to me and to you [cf. 1:24], Jesus, Son of God most high? I adjure thee by God [put Jesus on oath], that thou torment me not" (v. 7). "Do not begin to torment me" (ingressive aorist preceded by *mē*). The demon knew that it had nothing in common with Jesus, so expected punishment.

Jesus commanded the demon to come out of the man (v. 8). Then He asked his name. "Legion: for we are many" (v. 9). A Roman legion had 6,826 men. This figure should not necessarily be pressed here. The point is that "many" demons had possessed the man. Hence his wild condition.

The demons "kept on begging" (imperfect) or exhorting Jesus not to "send them away out of the country" or back into the abyss. Since they must leave the man, not wishing to be dispossessed completely, they asked to be permitted to enter a herd of two thousand swine feeding nearby (vv. 11-12). The eastern side of the sea was in the Decapolis, a region of ten Greek cities, so it was Gentile territory. Hence the swine.

Jesus permitted it. And the demonized swine rushed down a steep place into the sea, "and were choked in the sea" (v. 13). The imperfect tense of "choked" *(epnigonto)* shows that pig after pig choked or was drowned. Some see a problem here of Jesus' miracle destroying property. But are pigs more valuable than men?

Those feeding the swine ran and told of the event "in the city, and in the country" (v. 14). "And when they came to Jesus, and see him that was possessed . . . sitting, and clothed, and in his right mind: and they were afraid" (v. 15). They had feared the man, but now they feared Jesus and what He had done. Seeing what had happened, "they began to pray him to depart out of their coasts" (vv. 16-17).

The popular idea is that they cared more for pigs than for the man. However, nothing is said about these being the owners of the swine. They asked Jesus to leave because they were afraid. They were pagans who feared their gods or any supernatural power. They simply wanted Jesus to leave the area. They recognized Him as God or as one with supernatural power.

The healed man wanted to go with Jesus (v. 18). But He told him to "go home to thy friends. and tell them how great things the Lord hath done for thee" (v. 19). "Tell" is *apaggeilon,* akin to the word for "gospel." He had a gospel to declare.

"And he departed, and began to publish [*kērussein,* to herald or preach] in Decapolis how great things Jesus had done for him: and all men did marvel" (v. 20). "Marvel" is imperfect, they kept on marvelling. One can hope that they also believed this *home missionary.*

24. The Daughter of Jairus and the Sick Woman (5:21-43)

Jesus returned to Galilee where He was once again greeted by the crowds (v. 21). There came to Him a "ruler of the synagogue" *(archisunagōgōn)* named Jairus (v. 22). His "little daughter" *(thugatrion,* diminutive of *thugatēr)* was "at the point of death." Note the father's tender word for his child. Literally, she "has a last." She was in the last stages of a disease (v. 23). He prayed that Jesus would come and lay His hands on her to heal her. Jesus "went" (aorist, immediately) with him, followed by the crowd (v. 24).

At this point Jesus' trip was interrupted by a woman with "an issue of blood twelve years" (v. 25). Note Mark's *layman's language* to describe her. "Suffered many things by many physicians" (v. 26). She had spent all she had with no beneficial results. Rather she "grew worse." She had no money left, but her disease grew worse. Luke 8:43 says that she had an incurable disease; a physician's diagnosis.

She had heard of Jesus' healing power and saw in Him her only chance (v. 27).

"If I may touch but his clothes, I shall be whole" or healed (v. 28). Matthew and Luke say touch the hem or tassel of His garments. A superstitious faith, but faith nevertheless. Note the woman's timidity, ashamed of her condition.

"And straightway *[euthus]* . . . she felt that she was healed" (v. 29). A miracle. "Virtue" is "power" (*dunamin,* v. 30).

Jesus asked, "Who touched my clothes?" So many were pressing in on Him. So the disciples wondered at His question (v. 31). But hers was the touch of faith, not mere jostling about.

"He looked round about." His eyes swept the crowd (v. 32). The woman fell before Him, "and told him all the truth" (v. 33). She poured out her pitiful story of chronic suffering.

Jesus replied, "Daughter [*thugatēr,* cf. v. 23], thy faith hath made thee whole. Go in peace, and be whole of thy plague" (v. 34). "Go into *[eis]* peace." Jesus healed her body, and evidently forgave her sins.

At this point a messenger came from Jairus' house with sad news. "Thy daughter *[thugatēr]* is dead" (v. 35). She "died" *(apethanen).* Not in a coma, but dead. There was no hope, so why trouble Jesus further? "Be not afraid, only believe" (v. 36). "Stop being afraid, only keep on believing." The word had chilled the father's heart, but Jesus *gave* hope.

Jesus told the crowd not to follow Him further. He took only Peter, James, and John with Him (v. 37). This is the first mention of the inner circle (cf. 9:2; 14:33). They were privileged to see this tremendous miracle.

"Tumult . . . wept and wailed greatly" (v. 38). Hired mourners had turned the home into bedlam (cf. Matt. 9:23). "The damsel [child, *paidion*] is not dead, but sleepeth" (v. 39). Some see this as evidence of a coma. Jesus meant that she was not dead to remain so. *Sleep* was often used of death (cf. John 11:11-14; I Thess. 4:13). She was truly dead. "Laughed him to scorn" (v. 40). The imperfect tense shows repeated continued laughing or jeering. The verb prefixed by *kata* shows that they really laughed Jesus down. Robertson notes that such loud laughter was hardly appropriate for so solemn an occasion. The paid mourners were about to lose their pay.

After putting them all out, Jesus took the parents and inner circle into the house where the dead girl was lying v. 40). *"Talitha cumi."* These were Aramaic words: "Damsel . . . arise" (v. 41). "Damsel" means "little girl," twelve years old. She "rose up [aorist, a miracle], and walked [imperfect, went on walking about]" (v. 42). Those who saw it "were astonished with a great astonishment [*ekstasei,* ecstacy]."

"No man should know it" (v. 43). Jesus did not want the people excited unduly. Note that He ordered that the girl be fed. A miracle, but now she needed strength from food or natural care.

25. The Rejection at Nazareth (6:1-6a)

From here Jesus went "unto his own country" *(patrida)* or Nazareth. On the Sabbath Day He was teaching in the synagogue. The people wondered as to the source of His teaching, wisdom, and mighty works (v. 2). "Is not this the carpenter, the son of Mary, the brother of James . . . Joses . . . Juda . . . Simon? and are not his sisters with us?" (v. 3). Did He work by hocus-pocus?

Evidently after Joseph's death Jesus had worked as a carpenter until He began His ministry. Note brothers and sisters. Some see these as *cousins* or *children of Joseph* by a previous marriage. This is based upon the idea that Mary remained a perpetual virgin. But Matthew 1:25 refutes this. "Firstborn" (*prōtotokon,* Luke 2:7) shows that there were other children born to Mary after Jesus. These were Jesus' half-brothers and half-sisters by Joseph and Mary. "Offended" means "stumbled." The former neighbors of Jesus stumbled over their knowledge of His former life. They could not believe that He possessed such ability, wisdom, and power. It was the old story of a prophet not being honored among his own people (v. 4). Probably Jesus quoted a current proverb (cf. John 4:44). He could not be much because they knew Him! To them also no good thing could come out of Nazareth (cf. John 1:46).

Because of their lack of faith Jesus could work "not even one" *(oudemian)* miracle in Nazareth. He did heal a few sick folk (v. 5).

"Healed" renders *therapeuō* whence comes "therapeutic." The verb usually used for miraculous healing is *iaomai.* But at times these verbs are used interchangeably. Does *therapeuō* here mean healing by treatment rather than by miracle? It could mean either. But in the light of "not even one mighty work," healing by treatment seems likely. Certainly Mark means that Jesus' work in Nazareth did not equal that in other places. Not because of Jesus' inability, but because of their lack of faith. It is possible that those healed did have faith.

Jesus "marvelled" (wondered) because of their "unbelief" (*apistian,* no faith, v. 6a). Alas, what a lack of faith cost these people! Insofar as the record shows, Jesus left Nazareth never to return.

26. The Mission of the Twelve (6:6b-13)

This records another tour of Galilee (v. 6b). Afterward, Jesus sent the Twelve forth "by two and two" (v. 7). They had been taught; now they must try their own wings. Jesus empowered them to deal with demons. "Gave" is imperfect; He kept on giving them power as their tour progressed.

They had a hurried mission, and so were to travel light. "A staff only" (v. 8). Every traveller needed a walking stick. They were to wear sandals, but only one *coat* or undergarment *(chitōn).* Two would have implied luxury. They were to abide in one house in a given place, there being provided with food (v. 10). They were not to go from house to house eating and drinking. Theirs was a working journey, not a pleasure trip. Note in verse 8: "no scrip," knapsack or bag; "no bread"; "no money [small change of copper, brass, or bronze] in their purse" (belt or girdle). The workers were worthy of their keep.

Some would refuse to welcome them or hear their message (v. 11). They should expect hostility. It might be a home or a village. "Shake off the dust under your feet for a testimony [witness] against [to] them."

This was a Jewish gesture of judgment or contempt. When Jews left a Gentile or Samaritan area they did this. The statement about Sodom and Gomorrha does not appear in the best texts. But it is genuine in Matthew 10:15.

The Twelve in groups of two went out and "preached" (heralded) repentance (v. 12). The verb "preached" *(kērussō)* means to herald as for a king. Such should be obeyed as if the king himself spoke. These heralded for the King. Hence the judgment on those who refused to hear and obey. Also they "cast out" many demons and "anointed" with oil the sick, and "healed" them (v. 13). These verbs are imperfects, showing their practice throughout the tour. "Healed" renders *therapeuō* (cf. 6:5). In parallel passages in Matthew 9:35 and Luke 9:2 "heal" renders *therapeuō*. It would appear that the apostles healed by treatment.

27. The Death of John the Baptist (6:14-29)

The fame of Jesus had spread even to the palace of Herod Antipas. When he heard of Jesus' mighty works he said, "That John the Baptist was risen from the dead, and therefore mighty works do shew themselves in him" (v. 14). The Baptist performed no miracles (John 10:41). But Herod's superstitious nature figured that if he rose from the dead, he could do so. Herod's guilty conscience plagued him. Others saw Jesus as one of the prophets (v. 15). But Herod said, "It is John, whom I beheaded" (v. 16).

Evidently John's execution was a recent event. For news of it caused Jesus to end His Galilean ministry (cf. vv. 29-32; Matt. 14:12). Mark related here the cause of John's arrest and death.

Herod arrested the Baptist "for Herodias' sake" (v. 17). Herodias had been married to Antipas' brother Philip, a private citizen in Rome. On one of his visits there Herod Antipas had seduced her, and persuaded her to divorce her husband to marry him. John the Baptist denounced this evil union. "It is not lawful for thee to have thy brother's wife" (v. 18). Note "thy brother's wife." She was still his wife in God's sight (cf. Lev. 20:21). Had Philip died childless it would have been Herod's duty to marry her. But such was not the case.

"Herodias had a quarrel against him" (v. 19). Literally, she "had it in for him." She "desired" to kill him, but was prevented by Herod. "Desired" is imperfect, an abiding desire. "Herod feared [imperfect] John." His wife kept on desiring to kill John, but he kept on fearing him (v. 20). Evil as he was Herod recognized John as righteous and holy. "Observed" means "kept safe" (imperfect). Apparently Herod heard John preach even while in prison. And when he did he "did many things" or "was much perplexed" (imperfect). Nevertheless, "he heard him gladly" (imperfect). The imperfect tenses make the scene come alive. Herodias and Herod kept on doing these things.

But Herodias found her chance. It was at a feast on Herod's birthday (v. 21). All the military brass and other notables were there.

When feasting and drinking had set the stage Herodias sent her daughter (Salome) to dance before them (v. 22). It was doubtless a lewd dance designed to inflame drunken passions. Such a shameful display was almost unprecedented for a woman of rank, even of respectability.

"Ask of me whatsoever thou wilt, and I will give it thee" (v. 22). Herod even took an oath before all – "unto the half of my kingdom" (v. 23). It was a public promise made under oath. But made by a drunk man! Herod was a tetrarch, ruler of a fourth of a kingdom, under Rome. It was not his kingdom to give. It was alcohol, not sense, talking. He had fallen into Herodias' trap.

Salome asked her mother what to ask. "The head of John the Baptist" (v. 24). When Herod heard the request (v. 25), he became very sad. But rather than to back down on his oath before the group, he granted it (v. 26). The execution was carried out (v. 27). John's gory head was brought on a "charger," a large serving tray (v. 28). It was a gruesome viand presented to Salome. But it was a delightful *morsel* to Herodias. This tragic event took place at Machaerus, one of Herod's fortress-palaces just east of the Dead Sea. It is being excavated at the present.

John's disciples took his corpse and buried it (v. 29). Where? Nobody knows. And then they brought the sad news to Jesus (cf. Matt. 14:12). John lost his head, but saved his *life*.

28. The Report of the Twelve (6:30)

At about this time the Twelve returned from their tour, reporting what they had done and taught. They were jubilant about the success of their first tour without Jesus. Jesus doubtless was pleased with the report, but was saddened about the death of His faithful kinsman and forerunner.

III. THE PERIOD OF WITHDRAWALS (6:31–9:50)

With this Jesus changed the pattern of His ministry. It was one year before His death (cf. John 6:4). For about six months, early spring to early fall, A.D. 29, He led the Twelve on a series of four withdrawals from Galilee, returning there intermittently. Perhaps four reasons prompted these withdrawals: to escape the enmity of Herod and the Jewish rulers; to get away from the fanatical crowds; to rest away from the hot summer in Galilee; to teach the Twelve preparatory to His forthcoming death. They must understand His person and mission.

1. The Feeding of the Five Thousand (6:31-46)

This was the first withdrawal to the eastern shore of the sea of

Galilee. "Come ye yourselves apart into a desert [a deserted area], and rest a while" (v. 31). They were exhausted from their tour, and overly excited about it. Jesus was also tired. "They had no leisure so much as to eat." So they left by boat "privately" *(kat' idian)*. They went alone (v. 32). But the people surmised their destination and ran around the northern end of the sea to meet them on the other side (v. 33).

When Jesus saw them they stirred His compassion. "They were as sheep not having a shepherd" (v. 34). Their rabbis had not provided them with spiritual food. The fact that they had run around the lake proved this. They wanted to be with Jesus. One wonders if they were not lying around on the ground as exhausted sheep after their run. This was perhaps the scene that greeted Jesus when He "came out" of the boat. So He began to teach them. Exhausted as He was He would not neglect them.

Late in the afternoon the disciples came to Jesus with a problem (v. 35). The people "have nothing to eat" (v. 36). They were concerned, but note that they said, "Send them away, that they may... buy themselves bread" (v. 36). Let them feed themselves.

But Jesus said, "Give ye them to eat" (v. 37). "Ye" is emphatic as over against "themselves." Like so many Christians they raised the problem of finances. "Two hundred pennyworth" (v. 37) or two hundred *dēnariōn,* about thirty-four dollars but with a greater purchasing power than today.

Jesus told them to see what loaves were available. They reported, "Five, and two fishes" (v. 38). Barley cakes and dried fishes, food of the poor. They got this from a lad (cf. John 6:9). So Jesus had the people sit down "by companies." Literally, "garden beds garden beds." On the green grass their many colored robes looked like garden beds of flowers (vv. 39-40). This reflects Peter's vivid memory of the scene. Note Jesus' use of organization.

After thanks and blessing Jesus "brake [aorist] the loaves, and gave [imperfect] them to his disciples to set [present subjunctive] before them; and the two fishes divided he among them all" (v. 41). Literally, Jesus "broke [one can almost hear the brittle cakes snap] the loaves, and kept on giving them to his disciples that they may keep on placing them alongside them." He kept this up until all were fed. The cakes and fishes did not run out. As God by His natural laws provides food through plant growth, so Jesus by laws unknown to men multiplied the loaves and fishes.

A miracle may be defined as an act of God contrary to natural law as man knows it, but not contrary to laws known to God, which He performs in accord with His spiritual purpose. This was what happened here and in all of Jesus' miracles.

After all were filled (v. 42), "they took up twelve baskets full of fragments, and of the fishes" (v. 43). Not scraps or garbage, but unused food as Jesus provided it. All Gospels call the baskets a *kophinos,* a wicker basket. It was customary among Jews to leave uneaten food for the servers. So each of the Twelve had a basket full of uneaten food. "Five thousand men" (v. 44). Matthew adds "beside women and children" (14:21). So many more than five thousand.

Verses 45-46 report that Jesus "constrained" His disciples to enter the boat and sent them away. "While he sent away the people . . . he departed into a mountain to pray." Note John 6:14-17. Seeing the miracle the people tried to force Jesus to become a political-military-bread Messiah, in accord with popular expectations. Perhaps the Twelve had encouraged this. Some see Jesus' effort as to get the disciples out of this revolutionary atmosphere. Note the order: constrained or forced the disciples to leave; dismissed the crowd; went aside to pray. Did Jesus have to get rid of the Twelve before He could quiet and dismiss the crowd? Certainly the entire unhappy event led Him to slip aside and pray.

2. The Miracle of Walking on the Sea (6:47-52)

The disciples were rowing back across the sea toward Bethsaida. "Even was come" (v. 47). It was late evening, 6:00 P.M. on. The boat was about half-way across the sea. Jesus "was alone on the land." A beautiful scene, Jesus standing on the shore in the late twilight. His prayer vigil was over. The Twelve were distressed in rowing. A "contrary wind" or one in their faces, made rowing difficult. "Fourth watch" was from 3:00 to 6:00 A.M. This shows what slow progress they were making. "Walking upon the sea, and would have passed them by." Another miracle.

The disciples thought that they saw a "spirit" or phantom (*phantasma,* v. 49). Naturally, they "cried out." It was a shriek or scream of terror (*anekraxan*). So Jesus spoke to them. "Be of good cheer: it is I; be not afraid" (v. 50). Literally, "stop being afraid." "I" is emphatic in the Greek text. Literally, "I am." Note the "I am's" of Jesus.

Jesus entered the boat, "and the wind ceased" (v. 51). The aorist tense means that it ceased at once, not a gradual dying down. Another miracle. "Sore amazed" (imperfect). They kept on being so. Literally, "And they sorely kept standing outside themselves out of overflowing." Their amazement was so great that it overflowed. Strangely, they "considered not [did not understand]" the miracle of the loaves. Their hearts were hardened (v. 52). They had missed the point of it as had the crowd (cf. John 6:24ff.). So this series of natural miracles left them confused.

John's Gospel parallels the others in recording the miracle of the feeding. He alone records the event the next day in the synagogue in Capernaum when the crowds left Jesus. John recorded all of this to show that Jesus lost the Galilean crowds when He insisted on being a spiritual Messiah and Saviour, not just a worker of miracles. The die was cast. He would follow God's will even if it led to a cross.

Of note is the fact that Mark does not record Peter's effort to walk on the water (cf. Matt. 14:28ff.). Evidently Peter avoided this in his preaching. Naturally he wanted to forget it.

3. The Ministry at Gennesaret (6:53-56)

The plain of Gennesaret was about six miles south of Bethsaida. The contrary wind had driven them off course. "Drew to the shore" (v. 53). This means that they *moored* to the shore, either cast anchor or tied the boat to a post.

The people "knew" or fully knew *(epignontes)* Jesus. So they ran about after Jesus bringing their sick (v. 55). Wherever they went crowds swarmed about Him that the sick might even touch His garment. "And as many as touched him were made whole" (v. 56). Mark records this scene rather than the one in John 6:25ff. This evidently happened as Jesus was walking back to Capernaum.

4. The Rebuke of the Pharisees (7:1-23)

Back in Galilee Jesus was again confronted by the scribes and Pharisees (v. 1). They saw the disciples eating bread with "defiled" or "unwashen" hands (v. 2). One suggests that they were eating the bread left over from the feeding across the lake. They had *not dipped (aniptois)* their hands in water for ceremonial cleansing.

The Pharisees and other Jews did not eat "except they wash [dip, *niptō*] their hands oft" (v. 3). "Oft" should read, "Diligently" *(pugmēi)*. They scrubbed their hands and arms up to the elbow with clenched fists. *Niptō* was often used for washing parts of the body; *louō* was used of the entire body (cf. John 13:10). The purpose was not hygienic but ceremonial. One belief was that demons got on the hands and from there entered the body while they ate. Mark notes that this was a "tradition [things handed down] of the elders."

Another tradition was before eating to sprinkle *(rantizō)* their bodies after being in the market place (v. 4). This was in case they had inadvertently brushed against a Gentile. Also they *washed* (*baptizō,* dip, plunge, immerse) cups, pots, and vessels. "Of tables," or couches, is not in the best texts. One reason for this was lest some Gentile hand might have touched these vessels.

These things were "according to the tradition of the elders" (v. 5). They were purely ceremonial with no relation to hygiene. Jesus condemned these empty traditions by citing Isaiah 29:13 (v. 6). He accused them of forsaking God's law to practice the teachings of men (vv. 7-9). Specifically He cited Moses' commandment about honoring parents (v. 10). "It is Corban" (v. 11) or a gift. A man by saying these words could dedicate his property to God, while keeping it for himself during his lifetime. He might cancel it at will. But by such a *dedication* he was freed from using his property for helping his needy parents v. 12). Instances were known of bribing a rabbi, thus making a false claim to *Corban,* to escape this filial duty. Thus they made void God's commandment by their tradition (v. 13).

These words were spoken to the scribes and Pharisees somewhat privately. But then Jesus called the people to hear His lesson drawn from them (v. 14). He revealed the hypocrisy of His critics. "Nothing without a man . . . can defile him" with the eating. He is defiled by what comes out of his mouth, not by what goes into it (v. 15). All were challenged to hear with understanding (v. 16).

Later in a house Jesus explained this to the disciples (vv. 17-23). Food taken into the body does not defile or make common a man. It enters his stomach, not his heart. It goes through the body and is cast out. Mark notes that thus Jesus made all food clean (v. 19). This reflects Peter's experience at Joppa (cf. Acts 10:14-16).

It is that which comes out of a man which defiles him. A defiled heart produces all kinds of evil (vv. 22-23). Pure food and drug laws protect the stomach. Only God's truth can protect the heart.

5. The Syrophoenician Woman (7:24-30)

This records Jesus' second withdrawal from Galilee. "Tyre and Sidon," on the Mediterranean coast south of modern Beirut, Lebanon (v. 24). It was outside Jewish territory, a heathen area. But even here Jesus did not gain privacy.

He was accosted by a "woman. . . a Greek, a Syropheonician by nation" (v. 26). She was Greek in religion (pagan), Syrian in language, and Phoenician by race. Matthew 15:22 calls her a Canaanite, the people of such degraded religion that God commanded their destruction by the Israelites, lest they defile His people. No one could have been more non-Jewish. But she was a woman in need, whose daughter had a demon (v. 25). She "besought [imperfect, kept on begging] him that he would cast forth the demon out of her daughter" (v. 26).

But note Jesus' response. "Let the children first be filled: for it is not meet [fitting] to take the children's bread, and cast it unto the dogs" (v. 27). Jews called Gentiles or non-Jews dogs. However, Jesus used the diminutive form, not wild dogs but little house pets (*kunariois*). In essence God's blessings were for "children" (Jews) not for "little dogs" or their pets (Gentiles).

But the woman was both persistent and clever. She took up the figure of "little dogs." They did eat the crumbs from the children's table (v. 28). One can almost see children on the sly dropping morsels to their hungry pets. The woman did not ask to sit at God's banquet table, just to get a few crumbs which fell to the floor.

Her persisent faith was rewarded. "Go thy way; the devil [demon] is gone out of thy daughter" (v. 29). The perfect participle (gone out) shows a complete cure. The woman went home to find that it was so (v. 30).

How may one explain Jesus' actions and attitude? Some see Him as infected with narrow Judaism. But this is untrue to His nature or life. Or as testing the woman's faith. But it was already strong. Or that He was not yet ready to minister to non-Jews. However, He had done this many times.

Was not Jesus in a living parable embodying the narrow "tradition" of the Jews (cf. vv. 2ff.)? He taught the disciples a lesson by showing their ugly, narrow attitude in action. It was one thing to despise Gentiles in general. It was another to apply it to one poor woman in need. Jesus showed that even the most non-Jewish person is the object of God's love and grace.

6. The Healing of a Deaf Mute (7:31-37)

From this region Jesus went eastward "through the midst of the coasts of Decapolis," another Gentile territory (v. 31). This was His third withdrawal, staying out of Galilee. There He was confronted by a deaf mute (v. 32). Taking him aside Jesus "put his fingers into his ears, and he spit, and touched his tongue" (v. 33). This was done privately in order not to excite these pagan Gentiles. And He remembered the reaction of the people in Gerasa.

"Spit." Some ancients regarded spittal as possessing healing properties (cf. John 7:6). Jesus doubtless did not share this belief, since He more often healed without it. Perhaps He used touch and spittal as an aid to the man's faith.

"Be opened" (v. 34). "Straightway *[euthus]* his ears were opened [aorist of point action], and the string of his tongue was loosed" (v. 35). His tongue was regarded as bound or tied. "He spake plain" or correctly. "Spake" is an imperfect. The miracle was instantaneous. The effect was continuous. Despite Jesus' admonition that this miracle be kept secret, the people told it far and wide (vv. 36-37).

7. The Feeding of the Four Thousand (8:1-9)

Some see this as merely a confusion with the previous feeding. But both Matthew and Mark record both. And there are differences between the two. The former involved Jews, the latter Gentiles. Again a lesson in God's love and grace.

The crowd had been with Jesus for three days, and now had nothing to eat. It aroused His compassion (vv. 1-3). Again the disciples raised a question as to how they should be fed (v. 4). They apparently had forgotten about the previous feeding. So once again Jesus told them to check their resources. They found seven loaves and a few small fishes (vv. 5, 7). Note the difference in number of loaves and fishes.

Again Jesus used organization to insure that all should be fed (v. 6). So "they . . . were filled" (v. 8). This time there were seven baskets of food left. Here "baskets" renders *spuridas,* a food basket. At the other feeding the baskets were *kophinos*. The number fed here was "four thousand." A similar miracle, but under different conditions.

8. The Demand for a Sign (8:10-13)

Apparently Jesus returned to Galilee (v. 10). The place is uncertain, but probably was in Galilee. For "the Pharisees came forth" (v. 11). Matthew 16:1 adds "Sadducees." They now joined their theological opposites, the Pharisees, in opposing Jesus in Galilee.

The Pharisees accepted all of the Old Testament as Scripture; the Sadducees regarded only the five books of Moses as such. The former believed in miracles and the resurrection; the latter did not. Pharisees were highly nationalistic, desiring to restore the Israelite nation. Sadducees sided with Rome to protect their position of wealth and power. Yet they joined forces against Jesus.

They sought "a sign from heaven, tempting him" (v. 11). The Sadducees did not believe in signs at all. The Pharisees regarded Jesus' other miracles as *from earth*. "From heaven" implied some supernatural display which they could attribute only to heaven. Both groups doubted that Jesus could do it.

Jesus "sighed deeply in his spirit" (v. 12). It came from His deepest parts in revolt against such crass unbelief. "Why doth this generation seek after a sign?" Jesus wanted men to see beyond the signs to their deeper meaning. He did not want to be regarded simply as a wonder-worker.

Matthew 16:2f. records Jesus' reference to His contemporaries' ability to figure the weather, signs in the heavens. But the greatest *Sign* from heaven was among them, and they did not discern Him.

"There shall no sign be given" (v. 12). Matthew adds, "But the sign of Jonah," referring to His death and resurrection (cf. Matt. 12:38ff.). That would be His "sign from heaven." But even then they would not believe it. With this Jesus left Galilee again by boat, and crossed the sea of Galilee (v. 13). Thus He began His fourth withdrawal.

9. The Warning about Leaven (8:14-21)

"Beware of the leaven of the Pharisees, and of Herod" (v. 15). The disciples thought that He referred to a shortage of bread for the journey (vv. 14, 16).

Jesus was warning against *bad theology* and *bad politics*. But knowing the disciples' denseness He reminded them of the two miraculous feedings (vv. 18-20). Note both miracles. These alone should convince them that Jesus was not concerned about physical bread.

"Not yet" *(oupō)* did they understand the difference between Jesus' person and work and those of the world (v. 21). Before condemning the Twelve, do men today comprehend the difference?

10. The Healing of a Blind Man (8:22-26)

Bethsaida on the eastern shore of the sea of Galilee was called

Bethsaida Julias to distinguish it from the town by the same name in Galilee (cf. 6:45). It was in Bethsaida Julias that a blind man was brought to Jesus for healing (v. 22). Jesus took him by the hand and led him out of the town. He wished to avoid publicity. "Spit on his eyes" (v. 23; cf. 7:33). But Jesus also healed blindness without using spittal (cf. 10:49ff.). Since this was in Gentile territory the man probably needed this prop for his faith. Then Jesus asked if he saw anything.

"I see men as trees, walking" (v. 24). Literally, "I see men for I behold them as trees walking about." His vision was still blurred. He saw what looked like trees. But since they were walking, he knew that they were men. This is the only case of a gradual cure on the part of Jesus. No reason is given for it.

Then Jesus again placed His hands on His eyes. Literally, "And he saw thoroughly and was restored. and went on seeing [imperfect] all things clearly" (or "at a distance." (v. 25). He had perfect vision.

Then Jesus sent him home, forbidding him to re-enter the town or to tell anyone about it (v. 26). He was trying to escape excitement, not create it. But He did not neglect human need.

11. The Examination and Lesson at Caesarea-Philippi (8:27—9:1)

Jesus had made His way northward to the region of the city of Caesarea-Philippi near Mt. Hermon. It was called by this name to distinguish it from Caesarea on the Mediterranean coast. It was located in Iturea, a region ruled over by Herod Philip. Note that Jesus still avoided Herod Antipas. But his brother had no evil designs toward Him.

This was a likely spot for Jesus to test His disciples' understanding of Him. Caesarea Philippi probably had originally been Dan associated with Hebrew worship. Later the Greeks made it a center of worship of the pagan god Pan, said by them to have been born in a cave there. It had been called Banias or Panias. Herod the Great had built there a temple to Caesar Augustus. So it had the flavor of emperor worship.

Therefore, in this atmosphere Jesus asked, "Whom do men say that I am?" (v. 27). There were many popular conceptions of Him (v. 28). Then He asked, "But whom say ye that I am?" (v. 29). "Ye" is emphatic in the Greek text. "Ye" is contrast to others. Literally, "But ye whom me do you say to be?" It was important what they thought. Only about six months remained before Jesus' death. Had they understood His teaching about Himself?

Peter answered for the group. "Thou art the Christ" (v. 29). "Thou" is emphatic. "Thou and no one else [not Pan, Augustus, etc.] art the Christ." Matthew 16:16 adds "the Son of the living God." Luke 9:20 reads, "The Christ of God."

"Christ" is the Greek equivalent of the Hebrew "Messiah," the anointed one. It is the official title of the incarnate God. Jesus usually avoided this title since to the Jews it had a political-military connotation. The Twelve had this view also. Hence Jesus' word that they should not tell it to anyone (v. 30). The Twelve were not ready to preach that Jesus was the Christ. For they did not yet comprehend fully His nature. Even had they done so, such a proclamation at this time would have been misinterpreted by the people.

Now that the disciples had confessed His Messiahship, Jesus "began to teach them" as to its true nature (v. 31). Some hold that it was here that Jesus first realized that He would die and rise again. But from the beginning He had taught such by inference (cf. John 2:19, 22). He began to teach it clearly here or "openly" (v. 32).

"The Son of man [Jesus' favorite self-designation] must suffer . . . be rejected . . . be killed, and after three days rise again" (v. 31). "Spake" (v. 32) is an imperfect tense, meaning that He told repeatedly what would happen to Him.

A suffering and dying Messiah was contrary to the disciples' concept of Him. They were children of their age. So "Peter . . . began to rebuke him" (v. 32). Note the two uses of "began" (vv. 31f.). This suggests that as Jesus repeatedly told it, Peter repeatedly rebuked Him. Apparently Peter's mind froze on "be killed." He certainly did not object to "rise again."

Apparently Jesus turned His back on Peter. But He quickly turned around to face him and the others. He rebuked Peter. "Get thee behind me, Satan: for thou savorest not the things that be of God, but the things that be of men" (v. 33; cf. Matt. 16:17). Now instead of speaking God's revelation (v. 29), he spoke for Satan. He was merely parroting the popular idea of the Messiah, not declaring God's purpose for Him. It was Satan's temptation again to get Jesus to avoid the cross.

Rather than to avoid the cross Jesus offered His followers a cross. Literally, "If any one wills to come after me, let him deny himself [deny self-effort at salvation and self-comfort], and take up his cross, and follow me" (v. 34). One bore his cross to his execution. Be willing to die for me, said Jesus. To follow was to share experiences. So they must be ready to share Jesus' experiences as told in verse 31. There may be hardships, suffering, and death. But there is also the resurrection.

Then Jesus struck a balance of life (vv. 35-36). This is a paradox, but is true. "Life" renders *psuchē*. It was used of animal life and the spiritual principle of life. So there is an interplay of ideas. If one would save his animal life, he will lose the true meaning of life. But if one loses his life in doing God's will, he will realize the true life both now and forever.

"For what shall it profit a man, if he shall gain the whole world [its glory and riches], and lose his own soul *[psuchē]*?" or life in its fullest here and hereafter (v. 36). "Or what shall a man give in exchange for his soul?" (v. 37). Having lost it for the world, what will be legal tender with which to buy it back again? Impossible!

One's attitude and conduct toward Jesus now determines His attitude and conduct toward him in the final judgment (v. 38). And then Jesus said a striking thing (9:1). Note the solemnity, "verily."

"Some . . . that stand here . . . shall not taste death, till they have seen the kingdom of God come with power." In 8:38 Jesus spoke of His second coming. To what did He refer in 9:1? Certainly His second coming did not occur before some of them died. Some see this as referring to the Transfiguration (9:2ff.). But *all* not "some" lived beyond this. His death and resurrection? All except Judas saw this. This hardly fits "some." The same may be said about Pentecost.

To what event could He refer? Perhaps the destruction of Jerusalem and the temple in A.D. 70. "Some" but not all lived beyond this. Any such event was regarded as a coming of God into history. Jesus had been trying to liberate His disciples' minds from Judaism. With the fall of the city and temple Judaism ceased to be a great religious power. Thereafter, Christianity was freed from its hindrance to move freely into the world on its own. This seems to be that to which Jesus alluded in 9:1.

12. The Transfiguration of Jesus (9:2-10)

This probably took place on nearby Mt. Hermon. About 9,200 feet above sea level, this was the "high mountain" of Palestine (v. 2).

"After six days" (v. 2; cf. Matt. 17:1; Luke 9:28 says "eight days"). All refer to one week later, after the scene at Caesarea Philippi. Note the inner circle again: Peter, James, and John. "He was transfigured before them." Luke 9:28 says that this took place as Jesus was praying. It came as an answer to His prayer. "Transfigured" renders *metemorphōthē*. Note "metamorphosis." Jesus suddenly underwent a change in body. Note "before them." This happened at night (cf. Luke 9:32). Had this change happened previously as Jesus prayed alone at night in perfect communion with His Father? At any rate it happened here "before them" that they might see.

"His raiment became shining [glistening], exceeding white" (v. 3). This was not a light shining upon Jesus from without. "His face did shine as the sun" (cf. Matt. 17:2). It was Jesus' deity shining forth from within.

"Elias with Moses . . . talking with Jesus" (v. 4). Luke 9:31 says that they talked of His "decease" or exodus out of the world: His death, resurrection, and ascension. "Elias" (prophets) and "Moses" (law), the law and the prophets or Hebrew Scripture. They spoke of the same things about which Jesus had taught His disciples. It was no new idea, but divine revelation (cf. Luke 24:25-27). The disciples needed to learn this.

"Let us make three tabernacles; one for thee, and one for Moses, and one for Elias" (v. 5). It was not long before the Feast of Tabernacles (cf. John 7:2). Peter proposed that they stay in that heavenly place to observe the feast. Truly "he wist [knew] not what to say" (v. 6). And he said the wrong thing. Note that he placed Elijah and Moses on equality with Jesus.

"A cloud overshadowed them" (v. 7). Clouds form quickly on Mt. Hermon. But this was the Shekinah Glory, God's presence in a cloud. "This is my beloved Son: hear him" (v. 7). As at His baptism so here Jesus was God's beloved Son and well-pleasing to Him (cf. Matt. 17:5). God approved of what Jesus was doing and saying. "Hear him." Not pagan gods or Caesar, not the Pharisees, Sadducees, or Herod, not the popular voice as to the Messiah, not even Moses and Elijah. But hear Jesus and heed what He said!

Then the scene passed. They "saw no man . . . save Jesus only" (v. 8). This is both real and poetic. As they saw only Jesus, so they should hear and obey only Him.

On the way down the mountain Jesus told them not to reveal what they had seen "till the Son of man were risen from the dead" (v. 9). This was dynamite! Not until then could it be told. But they never forgot it. And after the resurrection they came to understand it, certainly Peter (cf. II Peter 1:16ff.; John 1:14; I John 1:1f.). The disciples "kept that saying with themselves" as Jesus had commanded. But they sought together to understand what He meant about rising from the dead (v. 10). They evidently missed the point in 8:31, but now they caught it even though it was still a mystery to them.

What was the purpose of the Transfiguration? Some say it was designed to encourage Jesus to go on to the cross. But there is no evidence that He ever entertained any other idea. Most likely it was for the disciples' benefit. They had failed, despite Jesus' teaching, to catch the point of His true person and mission. So He prayed for a heavenly demonstration so great that they would see Him truly as deity in the flesh, and that His true mission was taught in their Scriptures. They were not to *rebuke* Jesus but hear and obey Him. Jesus prayed, and His prayer was answered.

13. The Problem of Elias (9:11-13)

The appearance of Elias on Mt. Hermon raised a question. So the three disciples asked, "Why say the scribes that Elias must first come?" (v. 11). Come before Christ appears (cf. Mal. 3:1ff.). The three had just seen Elijah — after Jesus had come. So they were puzzled. But Jesus said that the prophecy about Elijah had been fulfilled, just as the Scriptures would be fulfilled about the Christ (v. 12).

"But I say unto you, That Elias is indeed come" (v. 13). Matthew 17:13 notes that they understood this reference as to John the Baptist. They knew both his work and his fate.

14. The Healing of a Demoniac Boy (9:14-29)

Jesus had left the other apostles at the foot of the mountain. So when He returned to them He found a scene of confusion. "A great multitude . . . and the scribes questioning" the disciples (v. 14). When Jesus arrived this was interrupted as the people flocked about Him (v. 15). Noting the embarrassed disciples He asked the scribes, "What question ye with them?" (v. 16). A man stepped out of the crowd to explain. He had brought his son to Jesus that He might heal him of an evil spirit. The son was *taken (katalabēi)* by a demon. The word "catalepsy" comes from this Greek word. Galen and Hippocrates used it for "fits." The demon "teareth him" or "dashes him down" or a convulsion. The boy "foameth, and gnasheth [grinds] with his teeth, and pineth away" or is limp. An apt description of such a seizure (v. 18). Failing to find Jesus the father asked the disciples to cast out the demon. But they failed. They had done so before, but not now.

Rebuking the disciples and others for lack of faith, Jesus said, "Bring him unto me" (v. 19). As the boy neared Jesus the demon threw him into another fit (v. 20). The scene is very personal as Jesus asked the father how long the boy had been in this condition. "Of a child" (v. 21) or, since he was a small child. Often in his fits the boy fell into the fire or water. "If thou canst do any thing" (v. 22), or "if thou may have power." He questioned Jesus' power in the light of the disciples' failure. The leper questioned Jesus' will (1:40), the father questioned His power.

Jesus threw the matter back to the father (v. 23). The idiom is lost in the translation. Jesus repeated the man's words. "The if thou may have power?" In effect, you question my power. I challenge your faith. "All things are possible to him that believeth." It was not a question of Jesus' power but of the man's faith.

The father caught the point (v. 24). He gave a loud outcry *(kraxas)*. "I believe. Help my unbelief." He had faith but also doubts. So he prayed for Jesus to remove the lack of faith *(apistia)*.

"Come out of him, and enter no more into him" (v. 25). It was to be a complete, permanent cure. With another convulsion of the boy the demon obeyed. The boy became limp as though dead. Many said, "He is dead" (v. 26) or, "He died." "But Jesus." Ah, there is the difference! *Seizing* his hand Jesus "lifted him up, and he arose" (v. 27). The aorist tenses show that it happened quickly. A miracle.

Privately the disciples asked, "Why could not we cast him out?" (v. 28). "This kind [evidently an unusual kind] can come forth by nothing but by prayer" (v. 29). "And fasting" is not in the best texts.

"But by prayer." This suggests that failure to pray had robbed them of power. Perhaps out of jealousy because they had not been taken into the mountain, they had been squabbling and complaining instead of praying. Had they followed Jesus' example in the mountain, they might have seen glory at the foot of it. Prayerless Christians are powerless Christians.

15. The Final Teaching in Galilee (9:30-50)

On the way back to Galilee Jesus continued to teach about what awaited Him in Jerusalem (vv. 30-31). The disciples still did not understand, and were afraid to ask for further explanation (v. 32).

Back in Capernaum, perhaps in Peter's house, Jesus asked, "What was it that ye disputed among yourselves by the way?" (v. 33). They had been debating about "who should be the greatest" in the kingdom (v. 34). This was a common thing among them. Jesus knew the subject of their jealous rivalry, but wanted them to admit it. But out of shame they held their peace.

"First . . . last . . . servant of all" (v. 35). One should be willing to be last if he would be regarded as first. And the lowest kind of a servant *(diakonos)*. In the world a man is considered greatest who is served by the most. In the kingdom of God the greatest is he who serves the most.

"A child" (v. 36). Simon Peter's child? To receive a little child is to receive Christ, yea, the Father (v. 37). Real greatness is caring about people, not necessarily important people, but people for people's sake. Such as a little child.

Thinking to change from this embarrassing subject, John pointed to his zeal for Jesus (v. 38). For his trouble he received a mild rebuke (v. 39). Anyone not against Jesus and His own is for them (v. 40).

Even a cup of water given in Jesus' name shall be rewarded (v. 41). Conversely anyone who causes a little one to stumble, child and/or a babe in Christ, shall be punished severely (v. 42). Speaking in oriental hyperbole Jesus said that it is better to go through life maimed than to be physically whole yet wind up in hell. "Hell" renders *geennan* (Gehenna), a place of punishment. Gehenna, the vale of Hinnom, was the garbage dump of Jerusalem. Worms ate the garbage. Fires burned constantly to consume it. Note "the fire is not quenched" *(asbeston,* "asbestos"). Jesus used this as a symbol of hell as a place of punishment. Except for James 3:6 it is used in the New Testament only by Jesus, the essence of love. Verses 44-46 are not in the best texts.

Verses 47-48 express the same idea. Note here that "worm dieth not" is used. But "fire . . . quenched" is not in best texts. But the two passages give a terrible picture of eternal punishment.

"For every one shall be salted with fire" (v. 49). The rest of this verse is not in the best texts (cf. Lev. 2:13). The meaning of this is uncertain. Jesus was talking about self-discipline before being a fit offering to God.

"Salt is good: but if the salt have lost his saltness, wherewith will ye season it?" (v. 50; cf. Matt. 5:13). Christians should retain their flavor for Christ and His work. "Have salt in yourselves, and have peace one with another." The disciples needed both of these exhortations.

IV. THE MINISTRY IN PEREA AND JUDEA (10:1-52)

1. The Lesson about Divorce (10:1-12)

Jesus left Galilee to return only briefly on His final journey to Jerusalem (cf. Luke 17:11). John records Jesus' visit to the Feast of Tabernacles (7:2—10:21) plus a visit to Jerusalem for the Feast of Dedication (10:22-39). In between these feasts Luke records a Judean ministry (9:51—13:21). Actually Mark's account begins Jesus' last journey to Jerusalem.

"The coasts of Judaea by the farther side of Jordan" was Perea on the eastern side of the river. Actually the Greek reads, "Into the border of Judea and beyond Jordan" (v. 1). It is inclusive of both Judea and Perea. The people flocked to Jesus here as they once had in Galilee.

And there were the ever-present Pharisees to harass Jesus. "Is it lawful for a man to put away his wife?" (v. 2). This they asked to tempt Him. Matthew 19:3 adds "for every cause." This explains the design to tempt or trap Jesus.

At this time there were two schools of thought among the Jews on divorce and remarriage. Hillel held to easy divorce "for every cause." If a man tired of his wife, she lost her beauty, burned his food — any cause — he could divorce her. Shammai held to the stricter view, divorce for only one cause, adultery. Hillel's view was the more popular. If Jesus did not champion it, He stood to lose favor with many men.

Jesus replied by asking as to the Mosaic law (v. 3). They referred to Moses' permission but requiring that a man should give his wife "a bill of divorcement" (v. 4). This was an improvement over the prevailing practice of sending a wife away with no record of divorce. Jesus did not make this the final word, but said that Moses did it because of the hardness of men's hearts (v. 5).

Then He went back to the beginning to point out God's original purpose in marriage (v. 6). Note "male and female." "For this cause shall a man leave his father and mother, and cleave to his wife; and the twain shall be one flesh" (vv. 7-8; cf. Gen. 2:24). "What therefore God hath joined together, let no man put asunder" (v. 9). Monogamy.

It should be noted, however, that Matthew 19:9 adds "except it be for fornication." Some question this. However, it has good manuscript authority (cf. Matt. 5:32). They argue that Mark does not have this exception clause (cf. vv. 11-12). But the exception was stated to the Pharisees in answers to "for every cause." Mark's account is stated privately to the disciples, and gives the ideal (v. 10).

Verses 11-12 include "and marry another." But the Pharisees' question implied remarriage. It may be assumed that here Jesus dealt with cases with no Scriptural grounds for divorce and remarriage. But the *exception* clearly implies the one ground for divorce and remarriage.

2. The Blessing of Children (10:13-16)

Jesus' teaching on divorce was interrupted by mothers bringing their little children to Jesus that He might touch them (v. 13). It was customary to bring children to the rabbi for blessing on their birthdays. Here was a special *Rabbi,* and the mothers wanted Him to bless them.

The disciples rebuked the mothers. For burdening Jesus? Or for interrupting the lesson? Probably the latter. They wanted to hear more. But Jesus rebuked the rebukers. "Suffer [permit] the little children to come unto me, and forbid them not: for of such is the kingdom of God" (v. 14; cf. 9:36f.). Blessed words!

"Whosoever shall not receive the kingdom of God as a little child, he shall not enter therein" (v. 15). "Shall not enter" has the strong double negative *ou mē*. Faith, obedience, simplicity. Children are not in the kingdom simply because they are children. But God's children should have these qualities.

So Jesus took the little ones in His arms (v. 16). He tenderly fondled them. And He "blessed them" (imperfect), one after another as He took them. Certainly a rebuke to the disciples, and a joy to the mothers. In later years the children would recall with joy that they had been held in the arms of Jesus to receive His blessing.

3. The Rich Young Ruler (10:17-22)

Jesus left the house (v. 10) to proceed on His way toward Jerusalem. A young man "came running" (note his eagerness) and "kneeled" (reverence) before Jesus (v. 17). He asked, "Good Master, what shall I do that I may inherit eternal life" or age-abiding life? He called Jesus "Master" or Teacher. "I do." He thought in terms of his work for eternal life.

"Why callest thou me good? . . . none but . . . God" (v. 18). God is absolute goodness. If Jesus was "good" He was more than a Teacher. Rather than denying deity Jesus inferred it. The man must first have a proper concept of Jesus.

What must he do? Keep the Ten Commandments *perfectly*. Jesus cited the last six (v. 19). But made no mention of the first four. The first four deal with man's relation to God; the last six with his relation to men.

"All these [the last six] have I observed from my youth" (v. 20). A good record, if true. Perhaps he had been negatively good by not doing some things. But what about positive good in using his wealth to help others? "Loved him" in Mark alone (v. 21). Jesus fell in love with him. He saw his potential. "One thing thou lackest." What? "Sell . . . and give to the poor." Not an oath of poverty. Here Jesus referred to the first four commandments. The man's possessions were his god, coming between him and God.

"He was sad" or "his countenance fell" (v. 22). His eagerness gave way to disappointment. "Went away grieved," but he went away. "For he had great possessions." He held on to what he regarded as life only to miss eternal life. He failed the test.

4. The Peril of Riches (10:23-27)

This sad experience prompted a lesson from Jesus. "How hardly." Not impossible, but difficult for a rich person to enter God's kingdom (cf. Matt. 19:23). He tends to rely on *things* rather than God (v. 24). This amazed the disciples who regarded wealth as a sign that one is pleasing to God. One cannot serve both God and mammon, but he can serve God with mammon.

Verse 25 may have been a current proverb for the impossible. There was no Needle's Eye Gate in Jerusalem through which a camel could enter only after being unloaded. The "eye of a needle" makes this statement more meaningful. One can enter God's kingdom only through faith in His Son.

"Who then can be saved?" (v. 26). If not a rich man, then who? It is impossible for man to save himself or other men, but "not with God: for with God all things are possible" (v. 27). If God willed He could push a camel through a needle's eye: head, hide, hump, hoof and all. God can save the most impossible case if he will receive His Son through faith.

5. The Matter of Reward (10:28-31)

This statement puzzled Peter. The young man had missed his reward. "We have left all, and have followed thee" (v. 28). Peter's boats and nets were small compared to the man's "great possessions." But it was *all* Peter had. What about his reward?

Verses 29-30 assure all who follow Jesus of their due reward. "Hundredfold" means complete reward now, and in the age to come. The figure should not be taken literally, but as a figure of speech. One will not have a hundred mothers or wives. Complete reward. It can be left with God to do right.

"First . . . last . . . last first" (v. 31). Since Peter and others had followed Jesus from the *first* would they have a greater reward than those who come *last*? Reward will not be reckoned by time or position but by God's grace and righteousness. There will be some surprises in heaven.

6. The Prediction of Jesus' Death (10:32-34)

Jesus was anxious to get to Jerusalem and what awaited Him there. Usually they evidently walked as a group. But now Jesus was "before," out in front of, them (v. 32). His entire attitude amazed the disciples. They "were afraid." For they sensed danger as they neared Judea, the seat of power of Jesus' foes.

So Jesus, sensing this, joined the disciples to tell them once again of His impending death in Jerusalem (v. 32). Note that for the first time He mentioned "Gentiles" or Romans (v. 33).

They will mock, scourge, and spit on Him, and kill Him. But on "the third day he shall rise again" (v. 34). Terrible ordeal followed by victory.

7. The Request for Prominence (10:35-45)

It was while Jesus was in this state of soul agony that two of His disciples made a crass request (vv. 35f.).

They were James and John, two of the inner circle. Matthew says that their mother joined them in the request (30:20). She was probably Mary's sister, Jesus' aunt. If true, the brothers were Jesus' first cousins. Which could explain the request.

"Grant us that we may sit, one on thy right hand, and the other on thy left hand, in thy glory" (v. 37). The places of first and second honor and power under Jesus in His kingdom. They still thought of an earthly Messianic kingdom. Keep it in the family. While Jesus thought of agony they thought of glory. This request is all the more shocking in the light of verses 33-34.

"Ye know not what ye ask" (v. 38). "Know" is *oidate*. They had not thought it through; they did not really know." "Drink . . . be baptized." These referred to death and suffering and all that they involved (cf. 14:36). "Baptized" here is used of being overwhelmed in sorrow and suffering. They were really asking for all this. Through the cross to the crown.

"We can" or "we are able" (v. 39). How glibly they answered, with no concept of what they were saying. In time they would indeed suffer (v. 39).

"For whom it is prepared" (v. 40). "Prepared" renders a perfect passive form. It had been prepared by another, God the Father. The perfect tense refers to a past action with continuing effect. Position in the kingdom is not something to be given upon a selfish request of the moment. God has set conditions which govern it. Suffering and service qualify one for such.

"The ten . . . much displeased" (v. 41). Not for the crassness of James and John. But that they had sought privilege above them. They wanted the same thing.

Jesus spoke to the Twelve about worldly, pagan and kingdom glory (vv. 42-44). Earth's standard of greatness is judged by how many serves one. Kingdom greatness is determined by how many one serves. "Whosoever may will to become great among you, let him be your servant" (v. 43). "Servant" renders *diakonos* (deacon), the lowest of slaves. "Chiefest [first] . . . servant [*doulos,* slave] of all" (v. 44). If one would rise to the highest place among men, let him be willing to occupy the lowest place among them.

Jesus Himself is the perfect example of this. "For even the Son of man came not to be ministered *[diakoneō,* verb form of *diakonos]* unto, but to minister [same verb], and to give his life a ransom for many" (v. 45). "Ransom *(lutron)* the price paid to free a slave or captive. This was not paid to Satan for the release of men's souls. It was paid to God to satisfy the demands of His holy, righteous nature. The ransom was "his life" or death. If the King achieved greatness in this way, surely His subjects may expect to suffer in their own degree and turn (cf. Phil. 2:5-11).

8. The Healing of Bartimaeus (10:46-52)

Jesus and His group had crossed the Jordan into Judea. "They came to Jericho . . . went out of Jericho" (v. 46). There were two Jerichos, old Jericho and the Roman Jericho. Jesus was between the two. "Blind Bartimaeus, sat by the roadside begging." Bartimaeus means "son of Timaeus."

He probably had heard that Jesus had healed the blind. "Jesus . . . son of David [Messianic title], have mercy on me" (v. 47). "Cry out" means a loud cry. This was his one chance, and he made the most of it. "Charged" or "rebuked" is imperfect. They kept doing this (v. 48). But he cried all the more. Jesus stopped and ordered Bartimaeus to be brought to Him (v. 49). Immediately casting away his outer cloak, he leaped up and came to Jesus (v. 50). It was a joyous moment for him. "Lord [*rabbouni,* rabbi], that I might receive my sight" (v. 51). Literally, "see again" *(anablepsō).* He had not always been blind. He wanted to see again.

"Thy faith hath made thee whole" (v. 52). "Hath saved" renders a perfect tense of *sōzō,* to save, to make well. Completely well. This could also mean salvation. "And immediately he saw again." The first thing that he saw was the glory of God in the face of Jesus Christ. It is no wonder that he went on following Jesus.

V. THE EVENTS OF PASSION WEEK (11:1–15:47)

1. The Royal Entry (11:1-11)

This is usually called the Triumphant Entry, the entrance of a king or conqueror into his capital city. But this entry was before victory not after it. Jesus came as a King of peace to His city. So His Royal Entry.

"Nigh to Jerusalem, unto Bethphage and Bethany" (v. 1). Located just over the crest of the Mount of Olives east of Jerusalem. John records previous visits of Jesus to Jerusalem (2:13; 5:1; 7:10; 10:22). These accounts explain the strong hostility to Jesus on the part of the Jewish rulers.

Jesus sent two disciples to fetch a donkey (vv. 1ff.). This suggests previous arrangements made secretly. Knowing the venomous purpose of the Jewish rulers, and Judas' attitude toward Him, Jesus moved with caution. He did not want them to know His plans or location ahead of events.

"A colt tied" (v. 2). Usually they ran loose. So apparently prepared beforehand. "The Lord hath need of him" (v. 3). Was this a prearranged signal? Things happened as Jesus had said (vv. 4-6).

Jesus mounted the donkey (v. 7). Evidently the people sensed what He would do. For they covered the donkey's path with their outer garments *(himatia)* and with tree branches (v. 8). They prepared a royal road for the King. Jesus was in the middle of a crowd (before—followed).

"Hosanna; blessed is he that cometh in the name of the Lord... hosanna in the highest" (vv. 9-10). As in Egypt the Jews expected that God would deliver His people at a Passover. The crowd expected Jesus to set up His kingdom at this time. They cried Messianic terms. "He that cometh" renders *ho erchomenē. Ho erchomenos,* the Coming One, was used of the Messiah (cf. Mal. 3:1ff.).

But Jesus simply entered the temple, looked about, and with the Twelve returned to Bethany (v. 11). The people doubtless were disappointed when their mistaken expectations were not realized. Jesus did not set up an earthly kingdom and proclaim war against the Romans. He came to Jerusalem as the King of peace, only to be rejected.

2. The Curse of the Barren Fig Tree (11:12-14)

The next day, probably before breakfast, Jesus returned to Jerusalem. "He was hungry" (v .12). Note His humanity. "A fig tree... having leaves... nothing but leaves; for the time of figs was not yet" (v. 13). Usually figs ripened in May-June. Perhaps in a sheltered spot this tree had leafed out, suggesting fruit. It promised, but did not perform.

"No man eat fruit of thee hereafter forever" (v. 14). A curse upon the tree. Why? This event forms an acted parable. Like the tree, Israel had promised to bear fruit unto God. Her outward emphasis upon religion was "nothing but leaves" with no *fruit.* Promise without performance. So this curse really was upon the Jewish-nation. She lost her place in God's purpose (cf. Matt. 21:43-45).

3. The Cleansing of the Temple (11:15-19)

Arriving in Jerusalem Jesus entered the temple *(hieron,* temple area, probably the Court of the Gentiles). "Began to cast out them that sold and bought... overthrew the tables of the moneychangers, and the seats of them that sold doves" (v. 15). Jesus had done this at the beginning of His ministry (cf. John 2:13ff.) Now the traders were back again.

This set-up, "The Bazaars of Annas," began as a service to the people, with the profits to go into the temple treasury. People coming from a distance, especially from outside Palestine, needed animals and doves to sacrifice. The temple tax had to be paid in Jewish coin, the half shekel. It was collected in the cities and villages up until about two weeks before the Passover. Thereafter it was to be paid at the temple. Those with Roman or other foreign coins had to exchange them for Jewish money, an exchange fee being charged. Gradually this *service* became a racket charging exorbitant prices, with much of the profits going into the pockets of those in charge. It was a scandal hated by the people, and repulsive to Jesus. So once again He threw this bunch out. Righteous indignation. Christians should be thus angered by some things.

"Would not suffer that any man should carry any vessel through the temple" (v. 16). The temple authorities had forbidden using the outer temple court as a short-cut to the Mount of Olives. This was disregarded. So Jesus enforced it. People should reverence the temple. Only Mark has this item.

Teaching following these events Jesus cited Isaiah 56:7; Jeremiah 7:11. "Of all nations the house of prayer . . . ye have made it a den of thieves" (v. 17). Gentiles seeking Jehovah would be driven away by the bazaar atmosphere in the temple area. Those doing business there were robbing the people. It was said that robbers and thieves even used the temple area as a place to plan their crimes. The holy area had become everything unholy.

In cleansing the temple Jesus had exercised authority which the Jewish rulers said belonged only to God, the Messiah, a prophet, or the Sanhedrin. His act was an affront to "the scribes and chief priests" (v. 18). So they "kept on seeking" or "began to seek" (imperfect) how they might destroy Him. Added to their purpose was their fear that He would upset their own place of power. For all of the people were amazed at His teaching.

"When even was come, he went out [imperfect] of the city" (v. 19). This day, and all other days. He would not be found in the city after dark. The first night spent in or near the city, He was arrested. So He *had the habit of going* out of the city, perhaps to Bethany or to some isolated place on the Mount of Olives.

4. The Lesson about Faith (11:20-26)

The morning after cursing the fig tree, it was found withered up "from the roots" (v. 20). Peter called attention to this (v. 21). From it Jesus taught a lesson.

"Have faith in God" (v. 22). Such faith could move mountains (v. 23). "This mountain" means a certain one and probably refers to the mountain upon which the temple stood, the seat of power of Judaism. Jesus may have pointed to it. The subtle thought is that He pointed to the time when the temple would be no more. The power epitomized by it would hound Jesus to His death. But His cause would survive the temple and what it represented. So despite what lay directly ahead for Him, the disciples were not to lose faith. He and they would prevail.

This led into a lesson on prayer (vv. 24-26). The disciples are in God's will to pray in faith and assurance. They are to forgive others if they expect to be forgiven when they pray to their Ftaher in heaven.

5. The Challenge to Jesus' Authority (11:27-33)

Back in the temple area Jesus was confronted by the Jewish rulers (v. 27). This day was one of controversy. The Jewish rulers were determined to break the hold that Jesus had on the people. Only thus could they hope to destroy Him. They had recovered from Jesus' onslaught the previous day. So they challenged Him to show "by what authority . . . who gave thee this authority to do these things?" (v. 28). They were within their right in asking this, since they were responsible for the temple. What was His authority, and who gave it to Him? Certainly they had not. They did not recognize Him as God, the Messiah, or a prophet. Hence their double-barrelled inquiry.

Jesus answered their question by asking one. If they would answer Him He would answer them (v. 29). "The baptism of John . . . from heaven, or of men?" (v. 30). Jesus did not act under John's authority or receive such from him. But since John the Baptist baptized Him, he was the only human source to which He could point. So what did they think of John and his baptism?

This put Jesus' antagonists in a dilemma. They "reasoned" (imperfect) for sometime among themselves. If they said, "From heaven," Jesus would ask why they did not believe John's message (v. 31). On the other hand, if they said, "Of men," they feared the people who held John to be a true prophet (v. 32). Either way they answered they were in trouble. Jesus often got them in this position during debate.

So they answered, "We cannot tell" (v. 33). Actually, "We do not really know" *(ouk oidamen)*. They retreated into agnosticism, the haven (?) of many who refuse to believe in Jesus. They knew about John from experience *(ginōskō)*. But they had not bothered to think through the matter to a firm conviction *(oida)*. If they had so superficial a knowledge about John, who were they to pose as judges of Jesus? So He refused to answer their question.

Actually, Jesus had by inference claimed authority from God or as the Messiah. But had He said so, they would simply have denied it. And used His claim as the Christ to accuse Him before Pilate as a revolutionist.

6. The Parable of the Husbandmen (12:1-12)

The time had come for Jesus to take off His *kid gloves* in dealing with these obstinate opponents. Due to their hard-hearted rebellion they had lost their opportunity to be used of God, both as rulers and as a nation. So they were cast aside. This truth Jesus stated in a parable.

The figure of the vineyard recalls Isaiah 5:1-7. Every preparation was made to provide a productive vineyard (v. 1). Then the owner leased it to husbandmen, and went away into a distant land.

"At the season" of harvest the owner sent a servant (*doulon,* slave) to collect his share of the grapes (v. 2). But with increasing violence they refused to give the rent (vv. 3-5). Note "beat . . . cast stones . . . wounded . . . killing." "One son, his wellbeloved, he sent him . . . they will reverence [respect] my son," the heir. "Let us kill him, and the inheritance will be ours" (v. 3). Strange reasoning, but they did it (v. 8).

What will the owner of the vineyard do? "He will come and destroy the husbandmen, and will give the vineyard to others" (v. 9).

Jesus applied the parable by citing Psalm 118:22f. (vv. 10f.). He is the stone rejected by the ones supposed to be building God's kingdom, but which God made the "head of the corner," the stone holding the walls together.

This was a parable of Israel as the wicked husbandmen. They refused to give God that which was due Him from His spiritual vineyard. They did to the prophets, sent to call them to honor their covenant, as described in the parable. Finally, God sent His beloved Son, and they soon will kill Him. So the vineyard (kingdom) will be taken from Israel and given to others, to Christians (cf. I Peter 2:4-10; Matt. 21:43-45).

The Jewish rulers knew that Jesus spoke of them. So they "kept on seeking" (imperfect) to seize Him to destroy Him (v. 12). However, they feared the people who were enthusiastic about Jesus. So they went away, biding their time until they had opportunity to carry out their evil designs.

7. The Question about Tribute (12:13-17)

Before taking Jesus the rulers had to show Him up before the people. They had failed to show His lack of authority. So in a series of confrontations they sought to discredit Him. The results were disastrous for them.

The first to try their hand was a coalition of Pharisees and Herodians (v. 13; cf. 3:6). After false praise they put a question to Him. "Is it lawful to give tribute to Caesar, or not?" (v. 14). Neither of these wanted to pay tribute to a foreign power. Their purpose was not to seek information, but to trap Jesus.

They thought they had Him in a dilemma. If He said, "Yes," they would accuse Him to the people as a traitor. If He said, "No," they would accuse Him to Pilate as a revolutionist against Rome.

Knowing their hypocrisy Jesus asked for a coin, a *dēnarion,* a Roman coin (v .15). The fact that they had such showed that they recognized Caesar's authority over them. "Whose . . . image and superscription?" (v.

16). On one side was the superscription and on the other the image of Tiberius Caesar.

"Render [give back] to Caesar the things that are Caesar's, and to God the things that are God's" (v. 17). One owes obligations to both. But they should not be in conflict. Taxes to Caesar; tithes to God. Neither should be used for the purposes of the other. The separation of Church and State. Each owes obligation to the other, but neither should control the other.

The tempters could only wonder and fall back. They retired to lick their wounds.

8. The Problem of the Resurrection (12:18-27)

It was now the Sadducees' turn at bat. They denied the resurrection (v. 18). Therefore, they tried on Jesus a problem with which they probably had often confounded the Pharisees who believed in the resurrection.

They cited the Mosaic law about a brother's duty to marry his brother's widow when he died childless (v. 19; cf. Deut. 25:5f.). Then they posed a problem of seven brothers who followed this law with all dying childless (vv. 20-22). "In the resurrection . . . whose wife shall she be?" (v. 23).

Jesus replied by accusing these experts on Scripture of ignorance of the same and of the power of God (v. 24). There is no marriage in heaven. All are the family of God (v. 25); "as the angels" who do not marry and produce offspring. As for death, those who die physically live on (v. 26). God is not the God of the dead, but of the living (v. 27). So the Sadducees erred in not understanding the Mosaic books which they accepted as Scripture. The Pentateuch taught life after death, a thing denied by the Sadducees. So this effort failed; it only showed the people what a brilliant person Jesus is.

9. The Question about the Great Commandment (12:28-34)

It was the Pharisees' turn again. So a scribe came to Jesus with a question as to "the first commandment of all" (v. 28). First in rank and in importance. So Jesus quoted Deuteronomy 6:4-5 and Leviticus 19:18b (vv. 30-31). The former had to do with absolute love for God (cf. first four of the Ten Commandments). The latter called for a similar love for one's neighbor (cf. last six of the Commandments). So they summarized the Ten Commandments. "None . . . greater than these" (v. 31).

The scribe commended Jesus for His answer (vv. 32f.). In turn Jesus said, "Thou art not far from the kingdom of God" (v. 34). What began as criticism on the scribe's part ended in praise for Jesus. The scribe was not in the kingdom, but near. One can hope that he entered the kingdom through faith in Jesus.

"No man after that [a double negative, *oudeis ouketi*] dared [imperfect tense] ask him any question." Jesus was complete victor over His critics. His hold on the people was stronger than ever before.

10. The Question about the Christ (12:35-37)

But He was not through. He sprinkled salt in the critics' wounds. "How say the scribes that Christ is the son of David?" (v. 35). True. Yet David had said by the Holy Spirit, "The Lord said unto my Lord, Sit thou upon my right hand, till I make thine enemies thy footstool" (v. 36; cf. Ps. 110:1). This is a Messianic psalm. So David called his *Son, Lord.* How could both be true (v. 37).

The point is that even though the scribes denied it, Jesus was/is the Messiah, the Lord. He did not claim it here, but implied it. The people the previous Sunday had proclaimed Him as such. And they heard Him not. One may well believe that both they and the scribes got the point.

This statement by Jesus involved both His humanity (David's son), and His deity (Lord). "The common people [not the scholars] heard him gladly" (v. 37). "Heard" is an imperfect tense. "The much crowd was listening gladly." They were delighted to see Him put the *scholars* in their place.

11. The Warning against the Scribes (12:38-30)

Jesus now turned to His disciples and the crowd (cf. Matt. 23). "Doctrine" is "teaching." "Beware of the scribes, which love to go in long clothing, and love salutations in the marketplace" (v. 38). Most of the scribes were Pharisees. Mark only summarizes a longer indictment of them found in Matthew 23. Since it was evident that they would not receive Him, but only keep others from doing so (Matt. 23:13), Jesus unveiled their hypocrisy in scathing terms.

"Beware," a warning to *look out* for them and their hypocritical ways. "Long robes" *(stolais),* the apparel of dignitaries such as kings and priests (v. 38). They made a great pretense, and coveted being saluted in public as great ones.

Also they "love" (*thelontōn,* the ones wishing for) "the chief seats" in the synagogues, and "the uppermost rooms at feasts" (v. 39). To show their piety they sat in the front seats. "Rooms" were couches. They wanted to recline on the couches of greatest honor. The Twelve were not immune to this (Luke 22:24).

"Devour widows' houses" (v. 40). This they did by getting them to give them to the temple, but actually took them for themselves. "Long prayers" as a pretense of piety. They preyed on widows, and prayed long prayers in public. For these things they will receive in the judgment a "greater condemnation." Jesus condemned hypocrisy to the utmost.

12. The Widow's Mite (12:41-44)

This is a beautiful ending to a day of controversy. With His antagonists gone, Jesus rested in the temple area. He "sat over against the treasury" (v. 41). It was in the Court of the Women. "Treasury" renders a compound word (*gazophulakeion,* from *gaza,* treasure, and *phulakē,* guard), a safe place in which to deposit money. In the Court of the Women receptacles were placed into which gifts for various purposes might be deposited (e.g., to buy wood used in burn offerings).

Jesus *was watching* [*etheōrei,* imperfect] as people cast money into these receptacles. The Lord of the treasury is concerned about the treasure given by His people. "Rich cast in much" or "were casting in much" (imperfect), a steady stream of givers. The "much" in contrast to the amount of the widow's gift.

"A [one] poor widow." "Poor" means a pauper, the extremely poor in contrast to the "rich." "Two mites" or *lepta,* worth about one-fourth of a cent. This was the smallest gift which, according to the scribes, was legal to give. In her case it was all that she had (cf. v. 44).

Jesus made no comment about the rich gifts. But calling His disciples, He said, "This poor widow hath cast more in, than all they which have cast into the treasury" (v. 43). More than the sum-total of the other gifts. He did not count the money, but weighed the love.

"Of [*ek,* out of] their abundance" (v. 44). They had plenty more left. This is the meaning of "abundance." "All that she had, even all her living" or livelihood *(bios)*. She probably went hungry that night. Note that Jesus did not forbid her to give. He would not deny her the privilege of expressing her great love for God. One should not say that he has given the "widow's mite" until he has given all that he has, even to the point of hunger. God measures gifts not by what one has before he gives, but by what he has left after he gives.

13. The Eschatological Discourse (13:1-37)

This is a most vital section, and calls for great care in interpretation (cf. Matt. 24-25; Luke 21:5-36; see my *Expositions of Matthew, Mark,* and *Luke,* Baker, Grand Rapids), on their accounts of this. As Jesus was leaving the temple area, never to return except as a prisoner, one of the disciples called attention to the grandeur of the buildings there (v. 1). Jesus' words to the scribes and Pharisees (Matt. 23:33-39) suggested that a great calamity would befall Jerusalem and the temple. This probably prompted the remark. "What manner of stones." The Herodian stones were large and well carved. Some may be seen there today. Josephus speaks of the size of these stones and the beauty of the structure. Surely nothing would happen to them!

But it would. "There shall not be left one stone [of the buildings] upon another" (v. 2). Only the foundation stones remain. This destruction occurred in A.D. 70 by the Romans. Recent excavations have been made revealing the destruction, including the ashes from the fired temple.

On the Mount of Olives overlooking the temple area Jesus and the Twelve sat down to rest from the exhausting climb. Peter, James, John, and Andrew came to Jesus "privately" (v. 3). Evidently they had been discussing His words about the fate of the temple.

"When shall these things be? and what shall be the sign when all these things shall be fulfilled?" (v. 4). Matthew 24:3 says, "When shall these things be? and what shall be the sign of thy coming, and of the end [consummation] of the world" or "age?" The disciples related the destruction of Jerusalem to Jesus' return and the end of the age. To them such a catastrophe could mean no less.

Before answering the questions of the disciples Jesus warned against false signs which could be related to His coming. "Take heed [beware] lest any man deceive you" (v. 5). "Deceive" renders *planaō* (note "planet"), to stray. The ancients thought of the planets as erratic, wandering bodies.

"Many shall come in my name. saying, "I am Christ, and shall deceive many" (v. 6). Literally, "saying, I am." These are not antichrists but false or pseudo-Christs. Every age has been plagued with such, and they always find a following.

"Wars and rumors of wars" (v. 7). It is amazing how many see these as a sign of Christ's return. He warned against such. "Be ye not troubled." Do not be disturbed, alarmed, terrified. Such things must be. They are merely a part of history, not a sign of the end of the age. "But not yet the end."

International turmoil and natural and social disaster are also a part of history (v. 8). "These are the beginning of sorrows" or "travail." As a woman in travail, they herald a better day to come. They are the birth-pangs of a new age to begin. Such will make men long for the end of the age and the new order under Christ.

Then Jesus said that rather than to be disturbed by these phenomena His disciples should be concerned about the immediate future, their own trials as they proclaimed the gospel. "Take heed to yourselves" (v. 9). By their Jewish enemies they will be "delivered" or handed over to the "councils" (*sunedria,* same word for Sanhedrin in Jerusalem; local councils were modeled after it). "Beaten" in the "synagogues." They will be flayed or whipped under orders from local Jewish congregations. These all suggest Jewish persecution up to A.D. 70. There is no record of such happening after this date.

Also they will be brought before "rulers [governors] and kings," or Gentile persecution, for Jesus' sake or their loyalty to Him and His cause. But their standing before them shall be "unto a witness to them." Their very patient endurance will testify of their faith. As indeed it did.

Parenthetically Jesus said that the gospel must be preached among all nations (v .10). Matthew 24:14 adds, "and then shall the end come." This was Jesus' one definite historic sign as to the end of the age. But it refers to *condition,* not *time.* His people should help prepare the condition, leaving the time to God (cf. v. 32).

Then Jesus returned to His theme. When persecution comes and they are brought before judging bodies, they are not to be concerned about a defense. The Holy Spirit will give them the words to say (v. 11). This reflects the early phase of Christianity before Christian doctrine had been formally worked out. Before A.D. 70? This promise is not related to sermon preparation but to persecution.

In such persecution Christians shall be betrayed by members of their own household (v. 12). This actually happened. "Hated of all ... for my name's sake" (v. 13). Jesus never promised that His people would be popular. Beware of courting such. Pagans even called Christians enemies of the human race. "Shall endure unto the end ... shall be saved." "Endure" (*hupomenō,* stand up under trial). The noun form *hupomonē* was a military citation ("patience") as well as an athletic term. Such was one who could take his opponent's onslaught, yet have sufficient strength with which to countercharge to victory. It does not here refer to keeping one's faith, but to enduring persecution without falling under it. "End" does not mean end of life, but end of the trial. "Saved" may read spiritual salvation, healing, or rescue from danger. The last probably applies here, with the first also as the end result. No matter what happens to the Christian, even death, he shall live on and be saved eternally. This puts no question on salvation but assumes it no matter what happens to the body.

Now Jesus began to answer the questions. The first had to do with the destruction of Jerusalem and the temple.

"Abomination of desolation" (v. 14). This reference is from Daniel (cf. 9:27; 11:31; 12:11). I Maccabees 1:54 relates it to Antiochus Epiphanes placing the altar to Zeus where Jehovah's altar was in the Jerusalem temple. Luke 21:20 relates it to Roman armies. This latter was apparently in Jesus' mind. "Standing where it ought not" or as Matthew 24:15 says, "stand in the holy place," the holy place or the altar of sacrifice in the Jewish temple. Jesus cautioned that one should understand His meaning (cf. Matt. 24:15). In Mark "the abomination of desolation" refers to a person.

However, there is no record of such in connection with the fall of Jerusalem. Coupling Mark's words with Luke 21:20 the reference seems to be to the Roman armies and their standards which represented Caesar. To the Jew the entire city of Jerusalem was "a holy place" (literal wording of Matthew 24:15). When these armies surrounded Jerusalem, that would be evidence that her fall was near.

Seeing this the inhabitants of Judea should "flee to the mountains." Get away from Jerusalem! The record shows that at this time

Christians fled to Pella in Perea (Eusebius). He attributed this act to knowledge of this word of Jesus.

Those on the "housetops," in the city probably watching the approaching army, should not go down into the house to get any clothes or food (v. 15). They were to flee by way of *the road of the roofs,* from housetop to housetop, until they were out of the city. Those in the field working, having laid aside the outer "garment" *(himation)* should not go for it, but should run for their lives (v. 16).

It would be terrible on pregnant women and those nursing children (v. 17). They would have difficulty in running. Also they should pray that their flight be not in "winter" (v. 18). The cold would bring added suffering with no shelter. Such suffering (*thlipsis,* to be in a tight place with no way out, like grapes in the winepress) had never been seen before, nor would such be after that (v. 19). "Neither" renders the strong double negative *ou mē. Not never* take place. So this does not refer to a *tribulation* at the end of the age. Jesus was talking about the destruction of Jerusalem in A.D. 70.

Had this condition continued over a long period no one would have survived. But for the sake of the Christians God made it of short duration (v. 20).

Now Jesus turned to the question as to His return and the end of the age. Again He warned about false reports as to His return.

"Lo, here is Christ or . . . is there" (v. 21). False Christs and false prophets will appear with a view to "seduce" or lead men astray (v. 22). "Signs and wonders" or miracles. Not genuine miracles but false pretensions at such, perhaps magic or other tricks. Such were prevalent just prior to the Jewish War, A.D. 66-70. And they have appeared through the ages, even today. "Believe. . . not" (v. 21). Do not trust in such.

"But take ye heed" (v. 23). In the Greek text "ye" is emphatic. Unbelievers might be led astray; "even the elect" or some Christians (v. 22). But these disciples in contrast to such should not be deceived. Jesus has told them in advance. This should apply to all who are familiar with His warning. Ignorance of the Scriptures makes many easy prey for those who abuse their meaning.

Then Jesus dealt with His second coming which will herald the end of the age (vv. 24-27). He used apocalyptic language which should not be interpreted literally but as expressing truth in vivid imagery. This was a form of writing used by Jews during persecution. They knew how to interpret it, but its message was hidden from their enemies. This was one vehicle used in prophecy of future events. Indeed, Jesus drew from prophetic language here (cf. Isa. 13:9f.; Ezek. 32:7f.; Joel 2:1f., 10f.; Amos 8:9; Zeph. 1:14-16; Zech. 12:12, Robertson, *Word Pictures,* Vol. I p. 377). There is no other way to express supernatural events which lie beyond and above history. "After that tribulation" (v. 24). "Tribulation" renders *thlipsis* (cf. v. 19). No word "great" with it here. Some see this as a period of trouble just prior to Christ's return. The writer sees it as covering all the sufferings of the saints in preaching the gospel through the ages. Whatever it means it will end when the Lord returns. Then will come great disturbances in nature (vv. 24f.). This was typical of apocalyptic language. One cannot be dogmatic as to its meaning.

"And then shall they see the Son of man coming" (v. 26). No secret coming, all shall see. Note that He will still be "the Son of man," God identified with His people, but "in great power and glory." "Gather together his elect" from everywhere (v. 27). Christ shall gather to Himself His own, not one missing.

In closing Jesus summed up both matters, Jerusalem's fall and His return. The former is seen in verses 28-31. As one can tell the approach of summer by observing a tree (v. 28), so he can know the approaching fall of Jerusalem (v. 29). "This generation shall not pass, till all these things [vv. 14-20] be done" (v. 30). Jesus did not return during that generation, but some living then did see the fall of Jerusalem about forty years later. Jesus almost set the date for this event. His words about it would be fulfilled (v. 31).

The same certainty as to the event applies to His return. But not the date. Of that time "knoweth [*oida*, really knows] no man, no, not even the angels ... neither the Son, but the Father" (v. 32; cf. Acts 1:7). The Son spoke what the Father told Him (cf. John 14:31; 15:15). And the Father has kept this *time* hidden in His own heart. This limitation of knowledge does not deny Jesus' *deity*. It emphasizes His *humanity*. Man cannot fully comprehend the incarnation. But in a way unknown to man Christ accepted limitations as He identified Himself with man, apart from sin. His knowledge was greater than that of any man. But He Himself stated this limitation, and it must be accepted as truth. There is no question as to this being genuine Scripture. But if Jesus did not know, man should be content not to know. The Christian's responsibility is to be busy establishing the *condition* (cf. v. 10), and leave the *time* with God.

Jesus did not expect His return to be in the immediate future (v. 34). He entrusted His "servants" with the stewardship of the gospel. They are to "watch" or constantly be on guard (v. 35). Jesus' return may be at any time: "at even ... midnight ... cockcrowing ... morning." These were the four watches of the night. So His servants are to be busy, not sleeping (v. 36).

"And what I say unto you I say unto all, Watch" (be on guard, v. 38). This is an abiding command.

14. The Plot of the Sanhedrin (14:1-2)

Having been defeated in debate on this Tuesday, the Sanhedrin determined to kill Jesus. The only answer to an unanswerable argument is violence.

"After two days was . . . the passover" (v. 1). This was after sunset on Tuesday, the beginning of the Jewish Wednesday. The passover began at sunset on Thursday or the beginning of the Jewish Friday. "Sought" (imperfect, were seeking). "By craft" or "in trickery." Their venomous purpose was to put Him to death.

"Not on the feast" or "in [during] the feast" (v. 2). They wanted to avoid "an uproar of the people." Originally they had planned to seize Jesus during the feast (John 11:57). But the crowd had shown its loyalty to Him at His royal entry and even on that Tuesday (cf. 12:37). So the Sanhedrin decided to wait until after the Passover when most of the people present would have left Jerusalem. They felt that they could handle the Jerusalemites, but not those from Galilee and elsewhere.

A Roman governor thirty years later took a census of the lambs slain at the Passover—250,000. Since one lamb was required for ten people, the number of people involved would be 2,500,000. This could well have been true at this feast. Hence the caution of the Jewish rulers.

15. The Dinner in Bethany (14:3-9)

That evening in Bethany "Simon the leper" gave a dinner for Jesus (v. 3). Perhaps he had been healed by Jesus. See John 12:1-8 for details such as names not given by Mark. The "woman" was Mary of Bethany. "Spikenard" was *nard,* a gift fit for a king. Cambyses gave such as a gift to the king of Ethiopia. "Poured . . . on his head." John says "feet," so both.

"Some . . . had indignation" (v. 4). "Why this waste?" A typical question by a worldly mind as to a spiritual service. John names Judas as the complainer, followed by the other disciples (Matthew). "Three hundred pence" or *dēnariōn* (v. 5), about fifty-one dollars. John adds that Judas cared not for the poor, but having the bag he wanted to steal it.

"Let her alone," said Jesus (v. 6). "A good work on me" (cf. v. 8). "Poor . . . always . . . but me ye have not always." She served Jesus while she could. "Anoint my body to the burying" (v. 8). Mary knew that Jesus would die (cf. Matt. 26:2). She had heard the report. So she asked, "What can I do for Jesus?" She anointed Him aforehand to show her great love. "A memorial of her" (v. 9). But for John it would have been an anonymous one.

When Mark wrote she probably was still living. To name her could have endangered her life. When John wrote she was already dead.

16. The Treachery of Judas (14:10-11)

John's account shows the immediate reason for Judas' act. Probably he had been disappointed by Jesus' actions following His Royal Entry on Sunday. Did he know of the Sanhedrin's latest plot (cf. vv. 1-2)? Certainly he heard Jesus predict the time of His death (cf. Matt. 26:2).

Rebuffed by Jesus at Simon's house he went straight from there to see "the chief priests" (v. 10).

His purpose to betray Jesus pleased them (v. 11). They had not counted upon treachery within the Twelve. So this changed their plans. "Promised . . . money." Thirty pieces of silver (Matt. 26:15; cf. Zech. 11:12), about twenty-five dollars. Failing to get the fifty-one dollars, he took what he could get. Note that the chief priests, not Judas, set the price. Evil pays its own reward. Knowing that Jesus would die, unlike Mary, Judas asked, "What can Jesus do for me?" And he betrayed Him for twenty-five dollars!

"And he sought [imperfect, kept on seeking] how he might conveniently betray him" or hand Him over to the chief priests for execution. He sought a *good time* to do this. Judas sold his *Master* for the price of a *slave*.

17. The Passover Meal (14:12-21)

All Jews were supposed to eat this meal. Jesus ate it with His disciples. "When they killed the passover" lamb (v. 12). The paschal lamb was slain at evening just before the beginning of the Passover (cf. Exod. 12:6). Preparations were made beforehand. So Jesus' disciples asked where they would eat the passover meal.

Jesus sent "two of his disciples," Peter and John (Luke 22:8), to make the preparations (v. 13). "A man bearing a pitcher of water: follow him." A man bearing water would be conspicuous, since this was usually done by women. This man would lead them to the house where the meal was to be eaten. Probably another secret arrangement by Jesus to keep Judas from knowing His plans. He would avoid betrayal until He was ready. Events were still in Jesus' hands.

"Guestchamber," literally, "my guestchamber" (v. 14). Loaned for the occasion, but with Jesus as host. A large upper room (v. 15), perhaps at John Mark's home. Furnished with carpets and couches. The actual meal was prepared by Peter and John (v. 16).

At the time for the meal Jesus and His disciples reclined on couches to eat (vv. 17f.). During the meal Jesus threw a bombshell among them. "One of you which eateth with me shall betray me" (v. 18). Note "one" not all. He did not name the betrayer, but spoke of the intimacy betrayed. "Is it I?" (v. 19). One by one they asked it. This question invited a negative answer. Matthew notes that eleven asked this question, addressing Jesus as "Lord" (26:22). None of them had thought of such a thing. But they were not sure as to Jesus' reference. Each hoped that He would say, "No."

In response Jesus repeated the idea of intimacy (v. 20). The betrayal must be, but "woe" to the betrayer (v. 21). Matthew shows that finally Judas, lest his silence betray him, asked, "Master [Rabbi], is it I" (26:25)? He also invited a negative answer, hoping that Jesus did not know. Or else he brazened it to the end. Note that Judas said,

"Rabbi," not "Lord." He was not a Christian. To him Jesus was just a rabbi. To Judas Jesus said, "Thou hast said."

Mark does not record Jesus' word to John privately, or Judas' departure (cf. John 13:23-30). But it happened at this point. Judas did not partake of the Lord's Supper. It is for baptized believers. He had been baptized, but did not believe.

18. The Lord's Supper (14:22-26)

After Judas left Jesus instituted this memorial supper. Jesus first "took bread," unleavened bread prepared for the passover meal (v. 22). After blessing and breaking it, He gave each disciple a piece. "This is my body" (v. 22). Not His actual body but symbolic of it. Not *transubstantiation* (bread becoming Jesus' body) or *consubstantiation* (body present with the bread), but a symbol. The same with the "cup" (v. 23); symbol of Jesus' blood (v. 24). The blood of the "new testament" or "covenant."

What were the contents of the cup? Was it wine such as was used in the passover meal? Was it a diluted wine? Or was it grape juice? The word "wine" is not used in any account of the Supper. The term is "the fruit of the vine" (cf. Matt. 26:29; Mark 14:25; Luke 22:18). Wine would be the fruit of the vine plus bacteria. Symbolizing Jesus' pure, innocent blood would it not, like unleavened bread, be free from such?

"I drink it new in the kingdom of God" (v. 25). The Jewish figure of the heavenly banquet. So the Supper points to the King's victory and eternal reign (cf. I Cor. 11:26). "Hymn" (v. 26). The Passover Hymn or Hallel composed of parts of Psalms 115-118. Mark notes that they went out to the Mount of Olives (Gethsemane). John records Jesus' words in Chapter 14. Then "Arise, let us go hence" (v. 31). There is no conflict. Mark simply notes that after they had finished in the upper room they went out to Gethsemane. He closed his account with 14:26.

19. The Audacity of Peter (14:27-31)

Robertson *(A Harmony of the Gospels)* places this event before the Last Supper, just after Judas' departure. He follows John's order at this point. Wherever it took place the meaning is the same.

Probably still in the upper room Jesus warned the Eleven that that night they would "be offended" or "be caused to stumble" because of Him (v. 27). However, He promised a reunion in Galilee after His resurrection (v. 28; cf. Matt. 28:7; Mark 16:7).

Peter protested. All the other disciples might stumble, "yet not I" (v. 29). He meant it at the time. But Jesus knew him better than he knew himself. "This night . . . thou shalt deny me thrice" (v. 30). In the Greek text "thou" is emphatic. Literally, "You today, this night, before the twice a cock to sound, three times me you will deny." Peter said that likely he alone of the group would not stumble. Jesus said, "You alone will deny me thrice." He did not merely stumble. He fell flat on his face.

But Peter, not to be outdone, said "the more vehemently" that he would die before he would deny Jesus (v. 31). "More vehemently" renders a strong compound word *ekperrisōs, ek,* out of, *perrisōs,* overflowing. He overflowed out, blurted it out. "Not" is a strong double negative *ou mē*. He could not have said it more emphatically. Poor Peter! But before condemning his audacity, note that the others said, "Amen!" How little people know themselves!

20. The Prayer Vigil in Gethsemane (14:32-42)

Just east of the city across the Kidron valley is the suggested Garden of Gethsemane. There or somewhere near was this garden in Jesus' day. *Gethsemane* means "oil press," perhaps in an olive grove. It probably belonged to a friend of Jesus. He often went there to pray (cf. John 18:2). It was sometime after midnight.

"Sit ye here, while I pray" (v. 32). This He said to eight of the disciples. Jesus' many mentions to watch or be on guard suggests that they were left as an outer guard at the gate. Until He was ready to be taken, Jesus did not wish to be disturbed. The inner circle Peter, James, and John, He took farther into the garden (v. 33). An inner guard? "Sore amazed . . . very troubled." This shows Jesus' burden as He faces the struggle in Gethsemane followed by the ordeal of the day ahead.

"My soul is exceeding sorrowful unto death" (v. 34). The burden almost killed Him there. "Watch." Be on guard. He went forward a little and "fell on the ground" (v. 35). The imperfect tense of "fell" shows Him falling. He did not kneel formally, but fell on His *face* so great was His soul agony. "Prayed." Imperfect tense, "began to pray" or "kept on praying." He did both. He prayed that if it *were* possible this hour might pass from Him. From the beginning He had faced it. Now He dreaded it. Not physical death, but more.

Note "Abba, Father" (v. 36). Both Aramaic, the language of His childhood, and Greek. *Abba ho patēr,* the definite article refers to both. *Patēr* was not a mere translation of *Abba* by Mark. In deep grief Jesus used both names for "Father."

"This cup." What does it mean? That He would not die in the garden? He knew He would not. Physical death? He had faced it constantly. He did not play the coward now. That He would not stay dead, but would rise again? He knew that He would rise again. What then? The "cup" was what His death involved, His becoming sin (cf. II Cor. 5:21). His pure, sensitive soul drew back in horror from such. If any other way to save man, but, if not, "nevertheless not what I will, but what thou wilt" (v. 36).

This was not a struggle with Satan. Or rebellion against God's will.

But a struggle in His own will that it might be in accord with God's will.

"Simon, sleepest thou? couldest not thou watch [stand guard] one hour?" (v. 37). Simon (not Peter the rock) had boasted of his loyalty. Thus Jesus addressed him alone.

"Watch [be on guard], and pray, lest ye [all three] enter into temptation [trial]" (v. 38). "Temptation" here probably means a testing or trial. If they did not stay alert the arresting group would come unawares. And in the test they would not be found genuine. So willing in spirit, but so weak in body. The late hour plus the strain had taken its toll.

Jesus went away and prayed the same prayer (v. 39). Returning He found them asleep again (v. 40). Shame and drowsiness made them speechless. Then the third prayer. "Sleep on now" (v. 41). No further need for guarding Jesus. "The hour is come." He was ready to be taken. Now that He had won the victory, He would drink the cup.

"He that betrayeth me is at hand" (v. 42). Perhaps Jesus heard them approaching.

21. The Betrayal and Arrest (14:43-52)

Judas arrived with the arresting detail. Since he had bargained with the chief priests, it was evidently temple police. "Staves" or clubs used by them (v. 43). "Swords" denote Roman soldiers, probably sent along to prevent a riot among the people. Judas' "token" or identification of Jesus was to be a kiss (v. 44). "Take" or seize. "Safely" means to lead away under guard. The safety factor was to be certain that Jesus did not escape. It had nothing to do with Jesus' welfare. Judas wanted to be certain of a successful arrest, and his own security in it.

"Master [Rabbi], and kissed him" (v. 45). Only one "Master" in the Greek text. Note again, Judas called Jesus "Rabbi," not "Lord." The kiss was probably on the hand, the greeting of a rabbi or teacher. Roughly they "took" or seized Jesus (v. 46).

One, Peter (John 18:10), "drew a sword . . . and cut off his ear" (v. 47). He aimed at the slave's head but he dodged expertly, losing only an ear. Peter had been told to guard Jesus (v. 34; cf. Luke 22: 35-38). Only two swords were necessary (Luke 22:38). Peter had one sword. Did the outer guard have the other (v. 32)? Peter did what he thought Jesus had ordered. Mark omits Jesus' healing of the ear (Luke 22:51) and His admonition to Peter (Matt. 26:52ff.; John 18:11). Jesus was now ready to be taken. Peter would get himself killed for nothing.

Jesus chided the band for coming after Him so greatly armed (v. 48). They could have taken Him in the temple any day (v. 49). But that would have precipitated a riot. Hence the night arrest. They did not know that Jesus would submit so easily. But He did that "the scriptures . . . be fulfilled."

"All forsook him, and fled" (v. 50). Where were their avowals of loyalty unto death? Mark alone notes the story of the young man (vv. 51-52). Was he that one? Perhaps the lad had been awakened when the band came to his house where the passover meal had been eaten. Wrapping a sheet about himself he followed them to Gethsemane.

22. The Jewish Trial (14:53-65)

Jesus was led away to the Sanhedrin (v. 53). Perhaps Nicodemus and Joseph of Arimathaea were not summoned to the meeting (cf. Luke 23:50). Peter "followed afar off" or from a distance. But He did follow (v. 54). Perhaps it was John who also followed, went with Jesus into the court of the high priest, and got Peter admitted to the courtyard of the palace (cf. John 18:15f.) "Warmed . . . at the fire." It was a cold spring night.

"To put him to death" (v. 55). Not a question of guilt or innocence, but to accomplish their purpose. False witnesses one after another testified against Jesus, but their testimonies were not the same (v. 56). The verbs in this verse are imperfects, showing a procession of such. Events had moved so rapidly that the *primed* witnesses had not arrived. So these evidently were pulled in without proper priming.

It seems that the prepared witnesses finally arrived (vv. 57-59). Evidently they had been told by the chief priests what to say (v. 58; cf. John 2:19). A misunderstanding or deliberate misuse of Jesus' words about the temple. This reference in Matthew (26:61) and Mark proves that Jesus cleansed the temple twice. But even these false witnesses did not "agree together" (v. 59). They did not tell the same story.

Jesus had remained silent. So the high priest asked if He made no defense against these charges, as though they agreed (v. 60). Still Jesus remained silent (v. 61). Why answer such ridiculous charges? And, besides, their minds were made up. The silences of Jesus during this and the Roman trial are significant. He spoke only to establish that He died as a King.

Then Caiaphas put Jesus under oath (cf. Matt. 26:63). "Art thou the Christ?" (v. 61). In Greek this called for an affirmative answer. "You, you are the Christ, the Son of the Blessed?" Though Jesus usually avoided using the title due to its current revolutionary connotation, He admitted to being the Christ (v. 62). To have said otherwise under oath would have been perjury.

"I am." The "I" is emphatic. "I and no one else am." But He added more. He added the word about His divine Kingship and second coming (v .62). This plus the "I am" was a definite claim to deity.

Illegally Jesus had been made to *incriminate* Himself (v. 63). So no other witnesses were necessary. Caiaphas accused Him of "blasphemy" because of His claim to deity (v. 64). "They all condemned him to be guilty of death." They *judged Him down* (*katekrinan,* to find guilty and pronounce sentence). It was a unanimous verdict, so illegal. Under Jewish law such should have been tantamount to acquittal.

Then followed abuse, also illegal; probably by the temple police. "Spit on him" (v. 65; cf. Isa. 50:6). Blindfolded, they began "to buffet" (strike with the fist) Him, and told Him to tell who did it—mockery. Servants also slapped His face. Insult upon insult. Evil was having its hour (cf. Luke 22:53). What was supposed to be a dignified, orderly court became a kangaroo court or mob scene.

23. The Denial of Peter (14:66-72)

All the while Peter was "beneath in the palace" or "court" (v. 66). Jesus' trial was in an upper area. "And thou also wast with Jesus of Nazareth" (v. 67). "Denied!" is an aorist tense, an instant denial. Literally "I neither know [*oida,* really know] nor understand what you are saying" (v. 68). Some manuscripts make the latter a question. "What are you saying?" The whole thing was preposterous. Mark notes that Peter "went out" or left the fire to get out of the light. "And the cock crew" (v. 68) is not genuine here, but is true in verse 72. Perhaps a copyist added it here to agree with "the second time" (cf. v. 30).

Later the maid said to those standing about, "This is one of them" (v. 69). Then a second denial (v. 70). Finally, several said, "Surely thou art one of them: for thou art a Galilean, and thy speech agreeth thereto" (v. 70). Galileans spoke a peculiar dialect.

That did it! The *rock* became *mud* again. "He began to curse and to swear" (v. 71). Some see "curse" as profanity. But the word *anathematizein* means to call down a curse on someone. "Swear" means to take an oath. So Peter called down a curse on himself if he was not telling the truth. Further, he took an oath about it. "I know not this man of whom you speak" (v. 71). "Know" is *oida,* to know perceptively. He did not deny any knowledge about Him, but a perceptive knowledge. In effect, he denied any intimate connection with Jesus. This was his third denial.

He heard the rooster crow (v. 72). And this recalled to him Jesus' words (cf. v. 30). "He wept" (*eklaien,* imperfect). He began to weep and kept on weeping. Matthew 26:75 says, "He burst into tears" (*eklausen,* aorist). A sad end for so boastful a beginning. Peter had the physical courage to defend Jesus. But he lacked moral courage to own Him.

24. The Roman Trial (15:1-21)

Under Roman law the Sanhedrin functioned in civil and religious matters. But it could not inflict capital punishment. So to obtain such they took Jesus before Pilate, the Roman procurator (A.D. 26-36).

The Jewish trial was held at night, which was illegal. So early in the morning they held a meeting to get around this technicality (v. 1). Even so, this was also illegal. They tried and sentenced Jesus on the same day. Jewish law required these to be done on separate days.

"Delivered" or handed over to Pilate for sentence and execution.

"Art thou the King of the Jews?" (v. 2). His question invited a positive reply. Among other things (Luke 23:2) the Sanhedrin had made this charge against Him. Since this had to do with His Kingship Jesus answered it. "Thou sayest." By inviting a positive answer Pilate had admitted it. "Thou" is emphatic. "You yourself say it."

But Jesus ignored further charges from the chief priests (v. 3). "Accused" is imperfect, kept on accusing. Pilate knew that Jesus was innocent of the charge. So he wanted Jesus to deny it (v. 4). But He "answered nothing" (v. 5). A strong double negative *ouketi ouden,* not anything. Pilate "marvelled" at Jesus' self-composure.

"Released" (imperfect), had the custom of releasing (v. 6). They did this on special occasions to placate conquered people. No other record of such in Palestine but Livy reports such elsewhere, so true here also. "Barabbas" (son of father, v. 7). "Murder in the insurrection." False messiahs when defeated by the Romans often became bandits. He evidently had been such (cf. John 18:40). Matthew 27:16 calls him "a notable prisoner." He may have been the leader of a band of robbers which included the two thieves (cf. Luke 23:33). So Barabbas may have been slated to die that day also.

The people demanded that Pilate release a prisoner (v. 8). Pilate wished to release Jesus, knowing that He was brought before him out of Jewish envy (vv. 9-10). Three times Pilate declared Jesus innocent of any crime (cf. Luke 23:4, 14, 22; John 18:38, 6; see also Matt. 27:24). Perhaps the people would have agreed. But the chief priests "moved" or "stirred up" (*aneseisan; seismos,* like an earthquake) the crowd to choose Barabbas (v. 11). Pilate hoped that they might also let him release Jesus (v. 12). "King of the Jews." Pilate grasped at this straw.

"Crucify him" (v. 13). This came with a loud cry, the whole mob. Still Pilate sought to release Jesus. His answer was an overflowing cry, "Crucify him" (v. 14). A Roman procurator pleading with a mob. Roman justice at its lowest ebb. Pilate had a bad record with the Jews. Rome would not abide a riot. So Pilate, to save his own skin, gave in to their demand (v. 15). "Scourged." Cruel punishment. The victim's back was bared, he was fastened to a post, and whipped. The many thongs had bone or metal in each end, so that chunks of flesh were beaten from the naked back. Customary before crucifixion, but here an innocent man.

The soldiers mocked Jesus (vv. 16-20). "Purple," royal color; but here probably a soldier's red coat (v. 17). A king must have a purple robe. "Crown of thorns"; long, sharp thorns. A king must wear a crown. "Hail, King of the Jews!" (v. 18). Usual way to greet Caesar. But here in derision. "Reed." A king has a scepter. But they beat Jesus with it. "Spit" (cf. 14:65). Mock obeisance ("worshipped"). "Led . . . out to crucify him" (v. 20), to Golgotha in a procession.

Due to the ordeal Jesus fell under the weight of His cross (v. 21). "Simon a Cyrenian." Probably a Jew from Cyrene in North Africa. "Out of the country." He probably spent each night outside the city and was coming in for the day. Mark alone mentions "Alexander and Rufus" (cf. Rom. 16:13). Was it this Rufus? Simon thought he was only walking into Jerusalem. But he walked into history as the one who bore the Saviour's cross.

25. The Crucifixion of Jesus (15:22-41)

"Golgotha . . . the place of a skull" (v. 22). "Golgotha," an Aramaic word meaning a mount shaped like a skull; Latin, Calvary. The location is uncertain. Not at the Church of the Holy Sepulchre. Outside the wall, but not definite as to wall's location. Some see it as Gordon's Calvary, outside the wall and shaped like a skull.

"Wine mingled with myrrh" (v .23). To deaden the pain of crucifixion. But Jesus refused it. He would suffer with a clear mind.

Crucifixion was the most agonizing of deaths. Naked, the victim's hands were nailed to the crosspiece, then lifted in place with the cross beam fastened to the upright. The feet were nailed to the upright with the body about two feet off the ground. In this strained position the victim hung. His rib cage stood out, blood gathered in his abdominal cavity causing great pain. The victim became terribly dehydrated, mouth dry, lips cracked, tongue swollen, and body fevered. Usually it took days to die. Crucifixion was forbidden for Roman citizens.

"Casting lots." The execution detail of four soldiers was permitted to divide the victim's personal effects. Jesus had only His clothes. Normally a Jew's clothing consisted of five things: sandals, headdress, girdle, outer garment, and inner garment. In this case each soldier took one each. But Jesus' inner garment was seamless (cf. John 19:23f.). Rather than to tear it they gambled for it (cf. Ps. 22:18).

"Third hour" was 9:00 A.M., Jewish time (v. 25). "Superscription" (*titlos,* John 19:19) was written on a board placed over the victim's head setting forth his crime. (v. 26). *THE KING OF THE JEWS* was Jesus' *crime*. Cf. John 19:20 for three languages: Hebrew or Aramaic, language of religion; Greek universal language of pagan culture; Latin, official language of Rome. Institutional religion rejected Jesus; pagan culture ignored Him; constituted government killed Him. All were there when they crucified the Lord!

"Two thieves" (v. 27). Probably companions of Barabbas. Was he supposed to be on the central cross? If so, Jesus was his *Substitute*. Verse 28 is not in the best texts. But see Luke 22:37 ("reckoned among the transgressors" means put on the list to be executed. Was Barabbas' name erased and Jesus' added?).

All the while the people jeered at Jesus (v. 29). They referred to the false witness (cf. 14:58), and said, "Save thyself, and come down from the cross" (v. 30). This was Satan speaking through the people.

He wanted Jesus to die but not on a cross, God's way to redeem men.

The chief priests and scribes evidently did not join the mob. Such would be below their dignity. Matthew and Luke might be construed that they did. But Mark alone says that their mocking was "among themselves" (v. 31). He saved others [cf. healing, raising from the dead]; himself he cannot save." This in response to the mob's cry in verse 30. The truth is that "He saved others; himself he *would* not save." "That we may see and believe" (v. 32). Satan's *voice* again. But they did not believe Jesus' resurrection, a greater miracle. "Christ the King of Israel" was spoken in mockery. The two thieves also joined in the reviling. But see Luke 23:39-43.

From noon until 3:00 P.M. there was darkness (v. 33). Nature rebelled at what was happening to nature's God. "My God, my God, why hast thou forsaken me?" (v. 34; cf. Ps. 22:1). Jesus cried out in Aramaic which Mark translated for his Roman readers. "Forsaken" may read "leave in the lurch." It is impossible to fathom the depths of suffering here described. Jesus now drank the full "cup," He became sin for man (cf. II Cor. 5:21). A holy God cannot look favorably upon sin. So for a moment he looked away that Jesus might bear the penalty for sin alone. He suffered the pangs of hell—God-forsaken. It was the infinite God suffering infinitely for the infinite guilt of finite man.

"Elias" (v. 35). Some mistook *"Elōi"* for "Elias." "Vinegar," a sour wine used by soldiers on detail.

"Jesus cried with a loud voice [cf. John 19:30], and gave up the ghost" (v. 37). He "expired." Matthew 27:50: "yielded up the ghost" or "dismissed his spirit." When His work was finished He said to His spirit, "You can go now." King all the way!

"Rent in twain from top to bottom" (v. 38). The temple veil between the Holy Place and Holy of Holies was torn in two, giving man unbroken access to God through Christ. Note "top to bottom," God's work, not man's.

"Truly this man was the [a] Son of God" (v. 39). Some see "a Son" as less than deity. But the Greek text reads literally, *Huios Theous* "God's Son." Note that every Centurion, commander of a hundred men, appears in a good light when mentioned in the New Testament.

"Women . . . afar off" (v. 40). An island of love in an ocean of hate (cf. also John 19:25). These women had been both blessed by Jesus and a blessing to Him (v. 41). "Followed" and "ministered" are imperfects. They had had the habit of doing these things (cf. Luke 8:1-3). They were held here by love. It is a beautiful ending to a terrible scene.

26. The Burial of Jesus (15:42-47)

It was late on Friday afternoon. Jesus had died about 3:00 P.M. Jews did not want dead bodies to remain on a cross on the Sabbath.

So their rulers requested Pilate to remove them before sunset, the beginning of the Sabbath (cf. John 19:31).

But others were also interested in the disposal of Jesus' body. All four Gospels record the story of Jesus' burial.

"Preparation" (v. 42). Mark for his readers identified this as the day before the Sabbath. It was the day when all necessary work was done (e.g., cooking) to make ready for the Sabbath. The Greek word *paraskeuē* in modern Greek is used for Friday.

"Joseph of Arimathaea" (v. 43). He was a rich man (Matt. 27:57), and an "honorable counsellor." A member of the Sanhedrin who had not agreed to Jesus' death sentence (cf. Luke 23:51). Since the verdict was unanimous, apparently he was not present when it was rendered. Evidently he was a secret disciple of Jesus (cf. Matt. 27:57). John links him with Nicodemus who evidently was also a secret disciple (cf. John 3:1ff.; 7:50ff.; 19:39). "Boldly" (v. 43). He was no longer afraid for his faith in Jesus to be known. And it took courage to befriend Jesus at this time. "Craved" means that he petitioned or strongly requested Jesus' body. Regarded as an executed criminal had no one claimed Jesus' body it would have been buried in potter's field, or thrown into Gehenna, the garbage dump of Jerusalem which Jesus used as symbolic of hell.

Pilate wondered if Jesus were already dead. Usually one did not die so quickly (v. 44). A centurion was called to determine the matter. The officer verified the fact (cf. John 19:32-37). So Pilate granted the request (v. 45). "Body" here means "corpse."

To prepare the body for burial Joseph purchased "fine linen" (v. 46). "Wrapped him in linen" with fine spices placed in the folds. John 19:39ff. gives greater details. "Hewn out" of rock. It was Joseph's new, unused tomb, located in a nearby garden (cf. Matt. 27:60; Luke 23:53; John 19:41). Joseph had prepared it for himself and his family.

Its location is not known. But it was near Calvary. See 15:22. Near Gordon's Calvary is such a tomb. A chapel of the Byzantine period was recently found near it, suggesting that it was regarded as a holy place. The left inside of this tomb is unfinished, which suggests that it may have been used ahead of schedule. "Rolled a stone unto the door of the sepulchre" (v. 46). To seal it a groove for such a circular stone is in front of Gordon's Tomb.

Mary Magdalene and Mary the mother of Joses beheld where Jesus was buried (v. 47). A tender ending to another sad, pathetic story.

VI. THE RESURRECTION OF JESUS (16:1-8)

1. The First at the Tomb (16:1-3)

Jesus' body lay in the tomb over the Sabbath. After the Sabbath, at sunset, certain women brought spices with which to anoint Jesus' body (v. 1). They thought that the hurried burial called for more spices. The women had no hope that Jesus would rise.

Early the next morning, Sunday, they came to the sepulchre (v. 2). "Who shall roll away the stone?" (v. 3). So great a stone was too much for them. "Said" (imperfect) shows that they discussed the problem on the way.

2. The Empty Tomb (16:4-6)

"The stone was rolled away" (v. 4). "Looked" means "Looking up." They had come with downcast eyes and hearts. But to their surprise the tomb was open.

"A young man" (v. 5). His apparel shows him to be an angel (cf. Matt. 28:5). "Sitting on the right side" in the tomb. As one looks into Gordon's Tomb the place for a body is to the right. "Affrighted." It renders a verb to be utterly amazed. Luke 24:5 has the verb to be afraid. Both ideas probably were true.

"He is risen" (v. 6). Crucified, but now risen. "Behold the place where they laid him." He was lying there but no longer (cf. Matt. 28:6, "lay," was lying). The angel did not remove the stone to let Jesus out, but to let the women in to see that it was empty.

Did Jesus stay in the tomb three days and three nights? Or three full days? Jews regarded any part of a day as a whole day. Friday before sunset (one day); Saturday (two days); Sunday before sunrise (three days). So the time element fits.

3. The Mission to Tell (16:7-8)

"Tell his disciples and Peter" (v. 7). Only Mark has "and Peter." Peter remembered with gratitude and joy this special notice of him, especially in view of his denials. Though Jesus appeared several times about Jerusalem during the next eight days, He had promised a meeting in Galilee. Two appearances were in Galilee (John 21; Matt. 28:16ff.).

Neither did they say anything to any . . . ; for they were afraid" (v. 8). This is the closing verse of the best manuscripts of Mark. A strange ending indeed!

VII. THE PROBLEM OF MARK 16:9-20

1. The Manuscript Evidence

In all likelihood these verses are not genuine Scripture. Such a position does not deny the authenticity of the Scriptures; neither does it take away any of the message. But it does clear up some problems. And there is nothing of truth found here that does not appear in unquestioned Gospel passages.

However, this is not an arbitrary position. It is supported by strong manuscript evidence. The two oldest and best manuscripts (Aleph and B) end with verse 8. Three other lesser manuscripts end here also. Some weaker manuscripts have a shorter ending than the one found in a large number of later ones, the ending found in the King James Version.

Robertson (*Word Pictures,* Vol. 1, p. 406) gives from Westcott and Hort the shorter ending found in "L." "And they announced briefly to Peter and those around him all the things enjoined. And after these things Jesus himself also sent forth through them from the east even unto the west the holy and incorruptible proclamation of the eternal salvation." The tone and wording show this to be the attempt of some later scribe to complete the story.

Some late manuscripts have both the long and short endings. The matter is quite complicated. But the evidence strongly argues against the ending found in verses 9-20.

An axiom in textual criticism is that where the differences in manuscripts occur the shorter and simpler is the most accurate. This is due to the human tendency to add to, not take from accounts. So on this basis alone Aleph and B may be regarded as more accurate than the others. As noted above on verse 8 that is a strange and abrupt ending. It does not complete the story.

Perhaps the original ending was lost. So various ones have endeavored to supply an ending. Someone wrote verses 9-20, and was followed by many others. But this passage safely may be regarded as not being the ending as Mark wrote it. However, since it appears in the text being used in this study, it will be well to examine it.

2. The Unbelievable Event (16:9-11)

Jesus' first appearance after His resurrection was to Mary Magdalene. This is reported in John 20:11-18. But when she reported it to the other disciples they "believed not" (v. 11). Some manuscripts said "they believed." Both are true. At first they did not believe (cf. Luke 24:11). But later they did believe (cf. John 20:8).

3. The Various Appearances (16:12-15)

Verses 12-18 obviously refer to the appearance to two disciples on the road to Emmaus (cf. Luke 24:13-32). However, "neither believed they them" is not true to the facts found elsewhere (cf. Luke 24:33-35; I Cor. 15:5). Verses 14-15 are a reference to Jesus' appearance to the disciples on the first Sunday evening and a later appearance in Jerusalem (cf. Luke 24:36-49; John 20:20-23). It also reflects Matthew 28:18-20.

4. The Problem Verses (16:16-18)

Verse 16a teaches baptismal regeneration. But 16b says nothing about being "damned" or condemned if one is not baptized. This within itself should raise a question about it. Furthermore, 16a is in conflict with the overall teachings of the New Tetsament that salvation is by grace through faith. One of the greatest theological battles of the first century was to prevent anything being added to faith and grace as necessary for salvation (cf. Acts 15; Rom. 4; Gal.; Eph. 2:8-10).

Passages usually cited to support baptismal regeneration may be interpreted otherwise. For instance, Acts 2:38 more likely reads "as the result [on the basis] of the remission of sins." Even "for" carries the same note. One is executed "for" murder, not in order to murder but because one has done so. The Greek preposition *eis* (for) may read *for, unto, into, on the basis of, because of, as the result of,* or *with reference to.* This last probably applies to Romans 6:3-4 ("into"). *Eis* in Matthew 12:41 is rendered "at." The Ninevites repented as the result of Jonah's preaching, not in order that he might preach. In I Peter 3:21 "baptism" is *baptisma,* not the act of being baptized but the meaning in the act, death, burial, and resurrection (cf. Rom. 6:3-4).

The Bible does not contradict itself. Where it may seem to do so, one should probe deeper, wait for more light, and/or interpret a given passage in the light of the certain teachings of the Scriptures. With regard to Mark 16:16 consult a sampling of such passages in John 3:16-18; Acts 15:11; 16:31; Romans 1:16-17; 3:23-26, 28-30; 4:3-5; Ephesians 2:8-10. Grace through faith and nothing else!

"New tongues" (v. 17) reflects post-Pentecost not pre-Pentecost. Jesus Himself never spoke in "tongues" in the modern sense of *glossalalia.* "Take up serpents . . . drink any deadly thing" (v. 18) certainly does not reflect the attitude of Jesus. "Serpents" may reflect Luke 10:19 and Acts 28:3ff. Luke 10:19 is a promise of God's keeping power, not a command to step on snakes and scorpions. Paul certainly did not deliberately handle a snake. One cannot from the New Testament support deliberate handling of snakes and drinking of poison as proof of one's faith. Jesus' words in Matthew 4:7 (cf. Luke 4:12) rather forbid one to put God to a test in doing dangerous things.

However, if one insists that baptism is necessary for salvation (v. 16), he should also handle snakes and drink poison to prove his faith (v. 18). The two hang together. But in the light of manuscript evidence the New Testament teaches neither.

5. The Ascension and Proclamation (16:19-20)

Verse 19 reflects Luke 24:51-53; Acts 1:9; Hebrews 10:12. And verse 20 summarizes early Christian history (cf. Acts).

This brief analysis shows that by discarding Mark 16:9-20 nothing of Christian truth is lost. But certain errors in the faith lose any semblance of scriptural support. It is not a question of believing or not believing the Bible, but of believing what the Bible really teaches.

Thus ends this examination of the Gospel of Mark (1:1—16:8). It is a terse, moving story of the greatest life ever lived. And it furnished the norm for other accounts to come (Matthew and Luke). Truly it is "the beginning of the [Gospels] of Jesus Christ, the Son of God" (1:1).